MW01688093

BEYOND THE READ ALOUD:

LEARNING TO READ THROUGH LISTENING TO AND REFLECTING ON LITERATURE

DOROTHY GRANT HENNINGS

25th Anniversary
EDUCATIONAL FOUNDATION
An Investment in Tomorrow
PDK

A Silver Anniversary Publication of
The Phi Delta Kappa Educational Foundation
Bloomington, Indiana

Cover design by Victoria Voelker

Copyright © 1992 by Dorothy Grant Hennings
Library of Congress Catalog Card Number 92-81539
ISBN 0-87367-458-8

To My Cousins and Dear Friends – Ralph and Ruth Hennings

TABLE OF CONTENTS

PREFACE

In 1979, Jim Trelease wrote *The Read Aloud Handbook* (Penguin Books). It became a nationally acclaimed best seller, and a revised edition appeared in 1989 as *The New Read-Aloud Handbook*. In this widely read book, Trelease recommends that parents and teachers read fine literature aloud to students. Trelease makes this recommendation not only to parents and teachers of preschool and primary grade children but to parents and teachers of students at all levels.

Today, more and more teachers are following Trelease's recommendation in the hope that students will learn to love literature and at the same time develop basic listening, thinking, and reading skills. Classroom teachers are sharing poems, stories, articles, and entire books orally with their students.

But as teachers include read alouds in their language arts programs, questions arise. Teachers are asking, "How do I organize a read aloud? What do I do before I share a piece so that there is a transfer of strategies and understandings to independent reading? What do I do while I share? What do I do after sharing?" In short, teachers are asking, "How can I get children to reflect on what they are hearing so that they become better listeners and, ultimately, better readers?"

This monograph focuses on reading aloud in the classroom and demonstrates ways to integrate read alouds into an ongoing whole-language program in which children learn to reflect on literature by listening and responding to it. It identifies and describes specific teaching strategies that invite students not only to listen to stories, poems, and nonfiction, but also to go beyond and think about what they are hearing, to talk about ideas, and to write in response.

In this book, you will meet three teachers: Ms. O'Dell (a kindergarten teacher), Mr. Wexler (a seventh-grade teacher), and Mr. Lugo (a fourth-grade teacher). These teachers are composites. I hope you will enjoy meeting Ms. O'Dell, Mr. Wexler, and Mr. Lugo and that you will be able to use some of their teaching strategies as you read stories, poems, and nonfiction to your students.

I thank all those who helped me to transform *Beyond the Read Aloud* from an idea into a reality. First, I thank Derek L. Burleson for encouraging me to write a second monograph for the Phi Delta Kappa Educational Foundation and David Ruetschlin of Phi Delta Kappa who served as project editor. It is always a pleasure to work with the professionals at PDK. I also thank teachers who tried out ideas in their classrooms and shared the outcomes with me. From teacher-researchers, I have learned much about what is effective in teaching.

And as always, I say a special thank you with love to my husband, George, who encourages me to put my ideas on paper, who helps to track references, and who reads and re-reads successive drafts of the manuscript. In many ways, this book is his as well as mine.

Dorothy Grant Hennings
January 1992.

1

LISTENING TO AND READING TEXT:

CONSTRUCTING MEANING

When people read, they do not simply "get" the message that an author wants to communicate. Rather, they reflect on an author's words and generate ideas and feelings in response. Good readers are meaning makers (Wells 1986). They make meaning by activating their prior knowledge of the topic, by anticipating and predicting, by raising questions and answering them, by visualizing, by inferring, by generalizing, by applying generalizations, by comparing and contrasting, by thinking of related examples, by organizing facts or concepts in some way, by feeling, by thinking critically and creatively, and by monitoring their understanding and their reactions as they proceed. Educators define this process as the active construction of meaning (Rosenblatt 1978; Rumelhart 1984; Tierney 1990).

Good listeners also are makers of ideas. Listening involves the reception and processing of incoming data. To listen is not just to hear; it is the active construction of meaning from all the signals – verbal and nonverbal – a speaker is sending. In this way, listening is closely akin to reading.

Reading, listening, and reflecting are closely related. By listening to and reflecting on literature, children and youth can acquire basic thought processes that are important for both listening and reading. Thus, students at every level should have numerous opportunities to listen to and reflect on stories, poems, and nonfiction.

This chapter will discuss four factors that affect the meanings that listeners and readers make with a text. It then will consider ways of constructing meaning – ways of reflecting on literature – that are common to listening and reading. Last, it will describe useful instructional strategies for integrating listening, reading, and thinking, as well as speaking and writing, in classrooms.

Making Meaning with Text

The constructive view of listening and reading sees meaning residing both in a text and in the listener or reader who interacts with it. The author of a story or poem has thoughts that he or she wants to share. Additionally, listeners and readers bring their own knowledge, feelings, values, and metacognitive strategies to the text; and these affect how they interpret it.

Both listeners and readers bring their prior knowledge to their reading of a text. This includes knowledge of facts relative to the topic, familiarity with concepts and related terminology, and understanding of underlying principles and generalizations. It also includes feelings about that content, such as the listeners' and readers' level of interest in the topic.

Another kind of knowledge that affects understanding is knowledge of the way the language works. For example, the position of the words in a sentence or the use of an apostrophe has meaning that must be learned.

A third kind of knowledge affecting what listeners and readers make with a piece of literature relates to the organization, or structure, of the text. For example, expository texts commonly have introductory segments in which the author explains what will be covered, what the main idea is, and how the selection itself is organized. Expository texts may have subheadings that break the selection into cohesive units, illustrations that parallel the development of the subject, and concluding segments that summarize. Story narratives generally have settings, characters, dialogue, conflict, a satisfactory resolution of the conflict, and a theme that ties the story together. Poems also have a design achieved through the use of repeating lines, pairs of rhyming lines, stanzas, and the layout of lines on a page. Knowledgeable listeners and readers use these elements of structure as aids to comprehension – to making meaning as they interact with text.

A fourth kind of knowledge is called *metacognition*. Metacognition is the awareness that listeners or readers have of strategies that help them make meaning from a text. For example, story listeners who keep asking themselves, "What does this story mean to me?" have a metacognitive strategy that facilitates their comprehension of the message. Similarly, readers who monitor their comprehension by going over major points after reading a segment and re-reading when they do not understand are applying a metacognitive strategy.

These four types of knowledge affect how a listener or reader will interpret a text. What they ultimately make with a text is as dependent on what they bring to that text as it is on what the author has put into it.

Ways of Reflecting on Literature

What kinds of meanings do listeners and readers construct? Communication specialists have identified basic cognitive processes important in comprehending a text, whether presented orally or in written form. These ways of reflecting include:

- Preparing by: activating prior knowledge, anticipating and predicting, and raising questions.
- Connecting by: visualizing and drawing, inferring, generalizing, applying generalizations, comparing and contrasting, thinking of related points and examples, organizing by arranging in a systematic or graphic way, and feeling.
- Extending by: thinking critically and thinking creatively.
- Monitoring comprehension.

Students should be engaged in these ways of reflecting as part of classroom listening and reading. To list these ways, however, is not to suggest that any particular way is more important, more basic, or more difficult than any other. Neither is it to imply that these ways of reflecting are discrete activities that listeners and readers carry out step by step. Preparing, connecting, extending, and monitoring occur together – parts of the whole that is called thinking.

Preparing by Activating Prior Knowledge. Think about what you do when you buy a book. You study the cover art, read the title, and read any introductory matter on the jacket or in the preface. If it is a nonfiction book, you probably think about the topic, relating what you see and read to what you already know. You also may consider what you know about other things the author has written or what friends have told you about the book.

For example, suppose you pick up the book, *All I Really Need to Know I Learned in Kindergarten* by Robert Fulghum. Reading the title from the perspective of a reading teacher, you may think to yourself: "Kindergarten . . . young children . . . important basic learnings to prepare for life. What do we hope children will learn in kindergarten? We have children listen to and begin to read stories, and we hope they learn to like them and to look at reading in a positive way. We involve children in social group activity, and we hope children learn to get along together. Those are probably the most important learnings in kindergarten. But there is lots more to learn beyond kindergarten!" And with those thoughts in mind, you begin the book.

Most readers and listeners have some knowledge of a topic or an author that they think about as they begin to read or listen to text. Such prior knowledge provides a framework for interpreting new knowledge. Many theorists propose that it is helpful to activate what one already knows by contemplating aspects of the topic before beginning. In short, readers and listeners must get themselves ready to think by thinking through relevant facts and ideas they already have. This is what is meant by activating prior knowledge.

Teachers can introduce students to strategies that help them to activate their prior knowledge. These preparatory strategies include:

- telling oneself: recalling facts and ideas on the subject;
- talking out: chatting with others about the meanings the subject holds for the listener or reader;
- brainstorming: free-association about the subject with words and ideas recorded randomly as they surface;
- webbing: free-association with words and ideas recorded in a web-like arrangement to highlight interrelationships;
- charting and outlining: organized, structured thinking about a subject with ideas recorded systematically as a chart with rows and columns or as an outline with topics and subtopics;
- drawing and writing: drawing pictures or writing sentences and paragraphs that summarize what one knows, believes, or feels about the subject.

In later chapters of this book, you will find examples that clarify these ways to activate what one knows before listening and reading.

Preparing by Anticipating and Predicting. Russell Stauffer (1980) was one of the first to stress the importance of prediction in comprehending a text. He proposed that good listeners and readers make predictions before and while they listen to and read a text. They make predictions based on what they already know about the subject and, in the case of reading, on what they discover by previewing the selection they intend to read. They listen or read to test their predictions – confirming, modifying, rejecting, and making further predictions as they proceed. In this way, predictions provide a purpose for listening and reading; they provide a framework that guides reflection.

Writers drop clues as to what they are going to say and how they are going to say it. Many of those clues are accessed easily by knowledgeable listeners and readers. For example, the title often hints at what a selection is about. Think about these titles from articles in a local newspaper. What would you expect to learn from articles with these titles?

"Latch-key Kids Need Activities"
"Budget Puts Squeeze on Colleges – Tuition Hikes Likely"
"Developer Admits Fraud Guilt"
"Dow Soars 45.50 in Spite of Witching Hour"

You probably can anticipate what the authors of the first three articles are going to discuss because you have considerable knowledge about those subjects. You may have trouble with the last if you are not knowledgeable about Dow Jones and witching hours. The point here is that ability to predict in a particular instance depends on the ability to activate prior knowledge about the subject.

Introductory remarks also provide clues as to where a writer is going. For example, in the introduction a writer may say, "I intend to cover the state of XYZ and then give four examples of XYZ in operation. I will conclude by explaining three ways that you can use XYZ in your work." Hearing or reading this, a person can predict rather precisely what is to come and can use that prediction to guide the listening or reading activity. The listener or reader may visualize, or mentally map, the structure of what is to come, using that anticipated structure to guide listening, reading, or taking notes (Sinatra 1986).

Some clues are nonverbal. Illustrations on the cover or front page, visuals scattered through the text, and boldfaced or italicized words are useful in making predictions before reading.

Stauffer (1980) proposed the Directed Listening-Thinking Activity and the Directed Reading-Thinking Activity as ways to involve students in predicting. In DL-TA and DR-TA, the teacher helps students to predict before listening and reading. As students listen and read, the teacher stops periodically to encourage them to test their predictions and to make more predictions as to what is coming. This instructional sequence has merit, for it demonstrates to young learners a strategy they can use to guide their independent listening and reading activity.

Preparing by Questioning and Answering. In 1961 Francis Robinson suggested that raising and answering questions while studying facilitates comprehension. Robinson devised the well-known study system, SQ3R, for handling expository text. In SQ3R, readers first **S**urvey the text they are going to read and write **Q**uestions based on major headings. They **R**ead to answer their questions and to formulate additional ones as they go along. Having read a segment of text, they **R**ecite the answers. Eventually, they go back to **R**eview, repeating the answers to questions they originally raised.

SQ3R was developed for expository text, but it can be modified for listening to and reading stories. In the context of listening, it becomes LQ-AS: Listen, Question, Answer, Summarize. Listeners continuously raise questions in response to a story. As they Listen, they keep their Questions in mind and generate Answers. Periodically, they Summarize what the author has said up to that point. LQ-AS puts the emphasis on active listening.

Readers of stories can apply a similar strategy: RQ-AS. As they begin to Read, they ask themselves a Question or two based on their general understanding of story structure. For example, they may ask, "What kind of a character is Matt?" and "How does Matt change through the story?" As they continue to read the story, they look for information that helps them Answer their questions; and they raise additional questions. Periodically, they stop to Summarize their answers.

Using such study schemes as SQ3R, RQ-AS, and LQ-AS, children and young people learn to raise and answer questions in a systematic way that aids comprehension. Having experienced these systematic study schemes, students begin to use automatically the twin processes of questioning and answering. As they listen and as they read, students process incoming data naturally and simply by formulating questions. And functioning in the way efficient and curious listeners and readers do, they continue to listen and read to find answers.

Making Connections by Visualizing and Drawing. When listening to or reading a description of some far-off place, have you stopped to picture it in your head? Visualizing in that manner makes a description come alive. It forces you to make connections between what you know about the world and what the author is telling you about that far-off place.

Read the following poem. As you do, visualize the scene that the poet, Alfred Lord Tennyson, has painted.

The Eagle

He clasps the crag with crooked hands;
Close to the sun in lonely lands,
Ringed with the azure world, he stands.

The wrinkled sea beneath him crawls;
He watches from his mountain walls,
And like a thunderbolt he falls.

To comprehend "The Eagle" is not simply to be able to repeat the details of the poem nor to raise and answer questions about it. Rather, to comprehend fully, one must recall everything one knows about eagles, crags, the azure world, the wrinkled sea, and thunderbolts; connect them to what Tennyson wrote; and then visualize a picture of what is happening in the poem.

The same is true with a story. Read this description of the Mad Hatter's tea party from Lewis Carroll's *Alice's Adventures in Wonderland.* As you read, visualize the scene.

> There was a table set out under a tree in front of the house, and the March Hare and the Hatter were having tea at it; a Dormouse was sitting between them, fast asleep, and the other two were using it as a cushion, resting their elbows on it, and talking over its head. "Very uncomfortable for the Dormouse," thought Alice; "only as it's asleep, I suppose it doesn't mind."
>
> The table was a large one, but the three were all crowded together at one corner of it. "No room! No room!" they cried out when they saw Alice coming. "There's plenty of room," said Alice indignantly, and she sat down in a large arm-chair at one end of the table.

In the picture you visualized, did you see only the details mentioned by Carroll: the table, the March Hare, the Hatter, the Dormouse, the arm-chair, and Alice? Did you also picture the teacups, the teapot, and the tablecloth? If you pictured more than the explicit details, you know how to visualize, to go beyond the text to build images in your mind.

Visualizing is as important for nonfiction as it is for fiction and poetry. Creating mental pictures is essential if one is to comprehend the design of the heart, the solar system, atoms and molecules, or the cell. In these instances, visualizing often takes a concrete form – the drawing of a diagram to clarify relationships. Because visualizing is so essential to comprehending what is heard or read, teachers must repeatedly ask students to paint pictures in their minds or to sketch them on paper until doing so becomes an automatic response to descriptions either heard or read.

Making Connections by Inferring. At times, listeners and readers must draw inferences. For example, they must infer from a character's actions or conversations the kind of person that character is and the way that character feels. Similarly, authors may imply reasons or causes – why a character did what he or she did. They leave it to listeners and readers to figure out why. To make the connection, listeners and readers have to ask themselves: "What kind of . . . ?" "How . . . ?" and "Why . . . ?"

P. David Pearson and Dale Johnson (1978) have defined three levels of meaning that arise out of an interaction with text: text explicit, text implicit, and script implicit. Text explicit meanings are stated directly in the words of the message. They require a minimum amount of personal interpretation. Take this statement as an example: Her eyes were the color of amber. To make meaning with it, listeners have to activate their knowledge of eyes, color, and amber and relate the color amber to eyes. However, they do not have to figure out what the author may have been implying.

In contrast, text implicit meanings are not stated directly in the words of the message. For example, consider this statement: Her eyes were bloodshot. The author of the statement does not tell explicitly why the eyes were bloodshot. Hearing these words, listeners have to recall from their prior experience that bloodshot eyes can have any number of causes: weeping, excessive use, a cold, or a more serious medical disorder. Based on the context in which the statement occurs, listeners or readers infer the cause.

To make script implicit meanings, listeners and readers must go far beyond the stated words to create meanings to which an author has barely alluded. For example, hearing the statement about bloodshot eyes, listeners may recall a great sadness of their own when their eyes became red from weeping. Hearing the statement, they may relive their personal sadness and remember the way their stomach knotted into a ball, their head ached, and their entire being suffered. As they listen, they think to themselves, "This is how that person must feel, too."

Sometimes in reflecting on these relationships within a story, listeners and readers may find it helpful to visualize connections (Bromley 1991). For example, they can use a simple character action web to make inferences about a character. Thinking actively about a story while listening to it, listeners write the name of a character in the middle of a "doodle sheet." Connected to the name, they write down things this character does. Connected to each of these actions, they doodle character traits – inferences as to the kind of person this character is. See Figure 1 for an example based on the book, *From the Mixed-Up Files of Mrs. Basil E. Frankweiler* by E.L. Konigsburg.

Listeners to and readers of stories often must make other inferences – inferences relative to time (What time of day is it? What year is it? What month is it? What is the season?), place (Where exactly is the story taking place?), and condition (Is it old? new? easy? difficult? weak? strong? How old is this character? How well-to-do are the characters?).

Making inferences also is important in listening to and reading factual material. Writers on current events, history, and science often force the audience to infer what they have left unsaid. Kinds of inferences listeners and readers must make are similar to those made for stories – inferences related to feelings, causes, conditions, characteristics, time, and place. A writer may even imply judgments, dropping clues about how he or she feels about an issue, person, or idea but not stating the judgment directly.

Why do writers imply rather than state directly? In some cases, writers of controversial material do not want to take a position, criticize someone by name, or risk a charge of libel. They may even be giving themselves the latitude to change their position at some future date. The result is that listeners and readers must make these connections for themselves. In short, they must think between and beyond the lines.

Making Connections by Generalizing. Most writers have a main idea that they hope to communicate. Novels and short stories have a theme; in a piece of expository prose, there is a thesis or overarch-

Figure 1. A character web of Claudia from the book, *From the Mixed-Up Files of Mrs. Basil E. Frankweiler.*

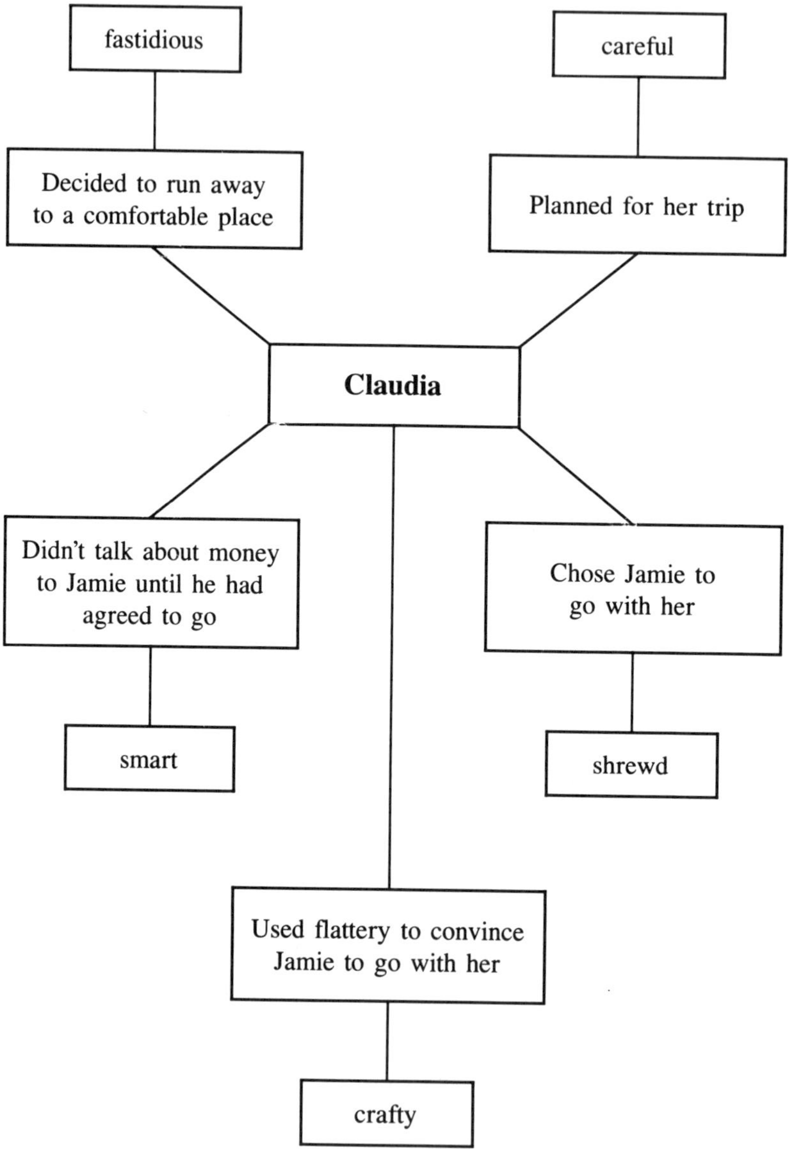

ing point. Sometimes this main idea is explicit, as in the case of a moral at the end of a fable. More often, however, a writer does not state the main thought, forcing listeners and readers to infer it from clues in the text. Listeners and readers must sift through the details and make generalizations. In generalizing based on specifics, listeners and readers are functioning as inductive thinkers.

To generalize, listeners and readers must keep in mind questions about the main idea from the very start and apply them as they sift through detail after detail. These questions are: "What is this author trying to say? What is he or she getting at?"

For example, suppose you are reading the newspaper column by Lawrence Hall titled, "The Wages of Syntax: Dictionary Reveals English's Bright Past, Potentially Dark Future." Before beginning to read, you consider the implications of the title. The title tells you that Hall's topic is the English language and the dictionary. But what point is he going to make? Thinking to yourself before reading, you use the title to anticipate what the author is going to say. You reflect, "I think that Hall is going to say that the English language is deteriorating."

Having targeted the main idea of the column based on clues in the title, you begin to read. Tracking the main idea as you read, you say to yourself, "Yes, Hall is concerned about language today. He is telling me that the future of the English language is bleak." But then in the third paragraph, you read, "the decline of the English language is linked to individuals and institutions that eschew a most basic book – the dictionary." Reading this sentence, you discover that Hall changes his focus and begins a discussion of the importance of the dictionary, quoting Samuel Johnson, citing Robert Browning, talking about Noah Webster, and describing the Oxford English Dictionary. As you encounter these details, you begin to modify your anticipated main idea. You think to yourself, "Hall is saying that the dictionary is a wonderful book; it is an important tool in understanding how to use the English language."

Finally you read the last sentence: ". . . it is incumbent upon us all to teach our children how to use the dictionary and to rely on it as a trusty friend in communicating with the world around them." Reading that last line, you – as a teacher – think out the *ultimate main idea*, "The dictionary is a wonderful tool in understanding how to use the English language with precision; we must do more with it in school programs." The ultimate main idea is what the column means to you.

As this example indicates, inferring main ideas is an ongoing process of generalizing based on details. Listeners to and readers of text use early clues – the title, information in a first paragraph, headings and illustrations in a written text – to target the main idea the writer has in mind. Targeting a point means anticipating or predicting the main idea before listening or reading. While actually listening and reading, people track the point by considering each new detail and by using the new input to modify their anticipated main idea. Coming to the end of a text, listeners and readers generalize; they invent the ultimate main idea – an idea that has personal meaning for them.

Making Connections by Applying Generalizations. Generalizations are powerful ideas. People use generalizations to solve related problems and explain related situations. In making this kind of connection, listeners and readers are functioning as deductive thinkers.

How does a listener or reader apply generalizations? To answer this question, let us suppose that you are listening to a speaker talk about ways to teach reading and writing. The speaker stresses that it is important to model reflective processes for students and that it is important to integrate reading and writing. Applying this generalization about instruction to your own teaching, you think to yourself, "Tomorrow I will follow the reading of the article on causes of the American Civil War with teacher-guided writing of a summary of the causes. Step-by-step and together, we will organize a paragraph; we will evolve a topic sentence with a main idea, and then we will draft several sentences of detail. In doing this, I will be modeling paragraph making; and I will be integrating reading and writing."

Cognitive processing of this type occurs often in the natural and social sciences. A student who has just heard about cohesion and adhesion is applying a generalization when she thinks to herself, "That explains why adhesive tape is called adhesive tape! When the tape sticks to a surface, two kinds of molecules are interacting. This also explains how we use the word adherent – a person who adheres to a particular belief."

Applying a generalization to solve a related problem or to explain a related situation is not easy. Listeners and readers must connect the generalization – the explanatory idea – to a situation with which they are familiar. To do this, they must perceive common features. Listeners, especially, must do this quickly if they want to keep alert to incoming data.

Making Connections by Comparing and Contrasting. Imagine listening to a television commentator talk about the budget deficit. Making a basic connection, you think, "That reminds me of my brother and his family, who spend much more than they earn. They live off their credit cards and pay only the minimum due each month. They are so deeply in debt, I don't know how they can ever dig themselves out. I don't know how our nation can ever get control of its spending, either."

Now imagine yourself reading a text. As you read, you think, "The way this author writes reminds me of the way Mr. X writes. Both authors use the same conversational style; both rely on specific examples to clarify theory."

Listeners and readers who make these kinds of connections are using analogy. They are identifying ways in which one item (person, topic, idea, mood, form, style) is similar to or different from another. They are relating a newly encountered and less-familiar item to something about which they are much more knowledgeable. By doing so, they are gaining control of new knowledge; they are making it their own.

Listeners and readers who make comparisons are building logical connections. Listeners and readers also can build creative comparisons. They can use simile and metaphor to come to a better understanding of a topic.

Thinkers create similes and metaphors when they identify a relationship between two items that does not exist in fact – when they compare two different kinds of things, often one that is abstract and one that is concrete. A simile is an explicit comparison that relies on the words *like* or *as* to connect the two items. A metaphor implies the comparison without those words.

To make similes and metaphors is to make the unusual connection – to find a personal meaning. This kind of thinking is at the heart of scientific investigation. Scientists make creative comparisons to clarify ideas. The same is true of poets. Poets play with similes and metaphors; and in the process, they help others to view the world from a unique perspective.

At times listeners and readers can try to unleash the force of creative comparisons. As they listen and read, they can think, "This is like . . ." and build an unusual analogy. In so doing, they must make a creative leap – one of the most sophisticated forms that thinking can take.

Making Connections by Thinking of Related Points and Examples. Closely akin to comparing is identifying related examples of a phenomenon being discussed. Hearing about duels many years ago in Europe, a listener may think, "There have been duels in the history of the United States and Canada, too. Alexander Hamilton was shot by Aaron Burr in a duel. In the Old West, gunfighters would challenge one another to a shootout."

To trigger this kind of reflection, listeners and readers ask the question, "What other examples of this phenomenon do I know?"

Making Connections by Organizing. To organize is to identify a pattern in the data, a pattern useful in interpreting what is still to come. In some instances this may mean developing a set of notes that highlights relationships in the text.

One way to organize one's thinking in response to a text is to identify sequential or chronological relationships. Reflecting on the order of events, listeners and readers may say to themselves, "This is what happened first, this second, this next, and this last." Or they may reflect, "This happened in the early nineteenth century, this in the mid-nineteenth century, this in the late nineteenth century." Perceiving these time relationships helps listeners and readers keep track of events. To facilitate their understanding, listeners and readers may jot down the events in sequence, perhaps organizing them visually as a time line.

A second way to organize one's thinking in response to a text is to identify hierarchical relationships based on the order of importance, significance, or complexity. Listeners and readers may conceive of a ladder and mentally (or on paper) place lower-order items on lower rungs, higher-order items on higher rungs.

A third way for organizing data is tabular. Listeners and readers slot data into the labeled rows and columns of a chart. Organizing in this manner generally requires taking notes and constructing a labeled table on paper. Early in the listening or reading experience, perhaps even before listening or reading the text, listeners and readers create the outline of the table and the labels that identify the rows and columns. They use the grid for taking notes while listening or reading. Collecting data graphically in this way helps in comparing and contrasting and in generalizing after listening or reading.

A fourth way for organizing data to highlight interrelationships is webbing or mapping. Listeners and readers link ideas together on a web-like drawing in which lines connect related data to a central hub – the topic of the selection. As they continue to read or listen, thinkers add more data to their webs, connecting them with strands to data already in place. An example of an idea web was shown in Figure 1 on Page 12.

Making Connections by Feeling. Reflection involves feelings, too. Listeners and readers may get emotionally involved in what they are receiving; they may feel happy, relieved, excited, surprised, sad, angry, tense, frustrated. By getting emotionally involved – feeling deeply about a topic – listeners and readers are making a personal connection with that topic.

Listeners and readers do not always control the feelings they generate in response to a text. An aspect of the text simply turns them on or off, striking a responsive chord somewhere deep inside them. But sometimes as part of reflection, listeners and readers trigger conscious consideration of their feelings. They ask themselves, "How do I feel? Why do I feel this way? Are my feelings preventing my understanding what this author is saying?" Asking these questions makes listeners and readers more aware of the personal biases – even prejudices – that affect their emotional response and their understanding of a message.

Extending by Thinking Critically. Barry Beyer (1988) has defined critical thinking as the process of judging the "authenticity, worth, or accuracy of something." He has identified 10 cognitive processes that are part of critical thinking – processes that listeners and readers use singly or in combination:

- distinguishing between verifiable facts and value claims;
- distinguishing relevant from irrelevant information, claims, or reasons;
- determining the factual accuracy of a statement;
- determining the credibility of a source;
- identifying ambiguous claims or arguments;
- identifying unstated assumptions;
- detecting bias;
- identifying logical fallacies;
- recognizing logical inconsistencies in a line of reasoning;
- determining the strength of an argument or claim.

Matthew Lipman (1988) also has emphasized the relationship between critical thinking and the rendering of a judgment by arguing that "critical thinking is skillful, responsible thinking that facilitates good judgment because it relies upon criteria." Criteria are "reliable reasons" on which listeners and readers found their judgments.

Bette Bosma and the National Council of Teachers of English Committee on Critical Thinking in the Language Arts (1987) have stressed the importance of suspended judgment in critical thinking. Critical listeners or readers are those who do not rush to render a judgment but rather wait until they have amassed considerable evidence in support of that judgment.

To think critically – to render judgments on the authenticity, worth, or accuracy of something based on reliable reasons and only after amassing considerable evidence – a listener or reader processes input by asking: "What is my opinion of this act, idea, story, happening, person? What evidence do I have to support my opinion? Is this evidence relevant? Is it enough to support my opinion? What are my beliefs that lead me to judge as I do?"

Dorothy Hennings (1990) has suggested that considerable knowledge relevant to the topic is necessary if a judgment is to be valid. She has described specific kinds of questions to ask in making judgments. These include questions about definitions, questions about background information, questions requiring projections and guesses relative to the topic, relational questions to help make connections, and ethical questions.

Implicit in this construct is the idea that to render a valid judgment, listeners and readers must know the meanings of the terms with which they are dealing, they must have considerable information on the topic, and they must have thought about that information in considerable detail.

Extending by Thinking Creatively. At times listeners and readers may jump far beyond what an author is saying to conceive original ideas of their own. In this case the author's words serve as a trigger that starts a new train of thought. Listeners and readers may stop listening to what an author is saying or they may halt their reading to ruminate on their own emerging thoughts. They may grab a pencil to jot down elements of the idea. The result is a personal invention – a creative idea.

Creative listeners and readers are ones who ask themselves, "What can I make with this? What can I do with what I am hearing or reading? Where do I go from here?" These are the "I" questions that encourage invention. They are questions that force listeners and readers to make connections between the messages they are receiving and their own knowledge, beliefs, and feelings. They are questions that lead thinkers to come up with something original.

Monitoring Understanding. Reading specialists emphasize the importance of knowing a number of ways to monitor one's reading and to use fix-up strategies when one has a problem. For example, a reader may reach the end of a section and think, "I don't get it." Knowing that he or she does not understand what the author is trying to say, the reader re-reads the section. Similarly, a reader may misread a word. Coming to the end of the sentence, that reader thinks, "That doesn't make sense," and goes back to self-correct.

It is more difficult to use fix-up strategies while listening. Listeners cannot stop to listen again; the oral presenter may already be into another aspect of the topic. However, listeners can monitor their comprehension by recognizing that they have failed to get a point. In general conversation, one strategy is to ask for immediate clarification by interjecting a question that requires the speaker to rephrase or repeat. During a formal presentation or an oral reading, a similar strategy is to jot down a question to ask at the conclusion or to pursue later on one's own.

Questions important in monitoring one's own comprehension in this way are: "What is this author saying? Do I understand it? Does it make sense?"

Listeners and readers also should keep alert for clues to where an author is going. Noting these clue words and phrases makes it easier to follow the author's train of thought. Examples of clue words include:

- phrases that tell how many points the author is going to cover ("I am going to make three points");
- sequencing words ("first," "second," "next," "after that," and "finally");
- words that introduce a related point ("and," "similarly," "in the same way," "additionally");
- words that introduce an opposite point ("but," "however," "on the other hand," "in contrast");
- words that introduce a reason ("because," "since");
- words that introduce an outcome ("as a result");
- words that introduce an example ("for example," "for instance").

For example, when a speaker says, "There are three ways environmental pollution affects the individual," listeners prepare to receive three ways. At the end, they ask, "Do I have the three ways?" By thinking like this, listeners as well as readers are setting up a framework for monitoring their understanding.

Teaching Reflective Thinking Behaviors

Good listeners and good readers can activate their prior knowledge, anticipate and predict, raise and answer questions, make connections, extend understanding through critical and creative thinking, and monitor their own understanding – all in response to a text they are encountering. Clearly, to reflect in these ways while listening or reading a piece of literature requires considerable mental and emotional flexibility. The listener or reader must process incoming data in several ways and draw on different cognitive processes.

How does a teacher help students to reflect as they listen and read? In this section, we will consider four instructional approaches: the read aloud, the literary conversation, the think aloud, and response writing.

The Read Aloud. There are four language arts: listening, speaking, reading, and writing. Reading aloud to children can involve all of these as well as critical and creative thinking. Through listening to fine literature, children learn the delights to be found within books and learn to reflect on the texts that they hear. The read aloud is the keystone of a language arts program that puts a high premium on student involvement.

Jim Trelease (1989*b*), one of the best-known advocates of reading aloud to children, argues that teachers should read aloud to children from the first day of school and that they should read to children in kindergarten to seventh grade. According to Trelease, reading aloud helps "to reassure, entertain, to inform or explain, to arouse curiosity, and to inspire." Experiences with books read aloud creates a "positive attitude about reading." Reading aloud "strengthens children's reading, writing, and speaking skills – and thus the entire civilizing process." Also, reading aloud helps children to become "better listeners and develop greater verbal skills."

Trelease suggests that teachers should practice reading aloud so they do it with ease; and they should preview what they plan to read to spot material they wish to shorten, eliminate, or elaborate. Before reading, teachers should set the stage for purposeful listening by helping children establish a purpose for their own listening. While reading aloud, teachers should sit in a comfortable position so that they can make eye contact with their students and their voices can carry to the far sides of the room. Teachers should use plenty of expression, changing tone of voice and pace to fit the message; and they should use their voices to communicate their personal interest in books.

The Literary Conversation. A second strategy for helping children to reflect on literature is the literary conversation, or what can be called the "literature talk out." Conversation is essential to learning (Shuy 1987; Genishi, McCarrier, and Nussbaum 1988). Through dialogue, young children become active speakers of their native language; they acquire the vocabulary, the sentence patterns, the nuances of vocal intonation, and the nonverbal elements that constitute their language.

Teachers can use the power of conversation to engage students in thinking about stories, poems, and nonfiction. Before students listen to a story, teachers can encourage them to talk about some of the early clues available to them. They can converse about the title and the clues the title provides about the topic, the characters, the setting, and the theme. They can talk about the illustrations in the same way. This also is the time to talk about the author and the kinds of things that author tends to write.

As teachers of young children read aloud, they stop at a few key spots for literary conversations. These brief pauses in a read aloud are times for listeners to talk about the predictions they made, to make additional predictions, to express feelings, and to ask questions.

Teachers can encourage young children to join in while listening. This is especially fun when a piece is filled with rhyming words and repeating lines. Teachers pause briefly before reading such a word or line and nod at the children as an invitation to join the storytelling. Young children love this. And there is more than fun to be had from joining in; students who join in are learning to anticipate and predict – to get out in front of the author to make meanings actively.

Young children should be engaged in oral reflecting after listening. Youngsters love to retell a story and talk about a favorite part, character, or picture. They also love to act out parts of a story, taking the roles of story characters and talking for them. Children enjoy playing with poetry by chorusing and singing along. When we think about a talk out, therefore, we are thinking broadly, not just in terms of conversations and discussions but in terms of creative drama and other forms of oral language as well.

With older students, teachers can stop periodically in the reading of lengthier pieces – for example, a novel being shared chapter by chapter – to converse with students. Literary conversations can focus on main ideas, reactions to those ideas, and relationships among characters and plot. They can briefly touch on feelings, mood, and tone. Older students also can re-enact scenes from a story and create extensions of it.

The Think Aloud. A third strategy for involving children in reflective thinking is the think aloud, which has its roots in the work of Lev Vygotsky (1986), who has described the relationship between thinking and language. According to Vygotsky, young children do a lot of talking aloud to themselves, a kind of speech that Vygotsky has called egocentric. With age, children's egocentric speech diminishes. But that does not mean that talking to the self disappears. It does not. Rather, young children begin to talk to themselves "in their heads"; also much of adult thought is verbal, sometimes called "mind talk."

Mind talk is tremendously important. David Corson (1987) has suggested that "There is every reason to believe that we speak inside and to ourselves more than we speak outwardly to others." Frank Smith (1982) has reported that of 29 adults he surveyed, all responded that they talk to themselves in their heads. Smith has suggested that talking to ourselves helps in the "organization of behavior, from constructing a mental shopping list to planning for the next few days, weeks or years." Talking to ourselves is an aid to clear thinking; it is a "mental scratchpad." According to Smith, mind talk also can be "emotionally supporting." We talk to ourselves when we are irritated, angry, sorrowful, as well as when we are elated and excited.

James Moffett (1983) has suggested that as we read and write, we modify our inner speech – our stream of consciousness. As Moffett explains: "Reading and writing temporarily change how we talk to ourselves. . . . When we read, we introject the text into our inner life and at the same time project our inner life into the text. This is heady interaction." The same is true of listening. When we listen actively, our heads are abuzz with thoughts – with mind talk. It is through mind talk that we process, or reflect on, messages we are receiving.

How do teachers help children to handle the mind talk that is the essence of reflective thinking? Many educators suggest that teachers orally model the kind of thinking they do while listening and reading by saying out loud the thoughts that go through their heads. Teachers make their inner speech public. In short, they think aloud.

Additionally, teachers should set up listening and reading opportunities that require students to employ the same cognitive processes they have modeled. They may read aloud to their students and ask them to talk out the thoughts that come to their minds. Or they may ask students to read aloud and simultaneously talk out their thoughts. In each instance, students are involved orally. It is through oral language activity that students learn how to use mind talk to make meaning in listening and reading.

Read alouds accompanied by literary conversations and by think alouds increasingly are being used as an instructional strategy for teaching children to make meaning while listening and reading. Some teachers share their mind talk as they read aloud and ask students to verbalize theirs. Others think aloud as they read the first paragraph or two of a selection and use those paragraphs to model the thinking students can do as they process the remainder on their own. By integrating language arts instruction in this way, these teachers are highlighting reflective processes common to both listening and reading.

Response Writing. A fourth strategy for helping students to reflect on literature is response writing. One device for encouraging writing after listening or reading is the literature response log, an ongoing journal for writing thoughts before, during, and after listening to, conversing about, and reading a text. Thoughts may be recorded as sentences and paragraphs, but they need not be. Some students may prefer a more visual record, such as a chart, a web, or a drawing.

As an example, after reading a chapter from a book, the teacher asks, "What is different in this chapter compared to the first one?" Rather than replying, students work in pairs to compile a chart of comparisons, which they write in their response logs. Later, students share their reflections with others by reading from their response logs. As they talk about their entries, students may be able to make connections.

After having collaborated in their response logs, students can write independently as they react to what they are reading. To do this, they first read a chapter for plain enjoyment. Then they stop at the end of a chapter to reflect – to make meanings. Again, emphasis is on reflection, not on writing full-blown paragraphs. Also, the emphasis is on using response logs as notes during follow-up conversations.

A teacher can guide the students in writing their responses to literature. This is especially appropriate when youngsters have had little or no prior experience in writing down their thoughts in response to stories, poems, or nonfiction selections. For example, after reading *Horton Hatches the Egg* by Dr. Seuss, a teacher may ask, "Do you like Horton?" Students express their opinions of Horton in a sentence that becomes the first in a response paragraph they dictate to the teacher. The teacher encourages further reflection by asking, "Why do we like Horton?" Children's reasons become supporting detail sentences in their cooperatively devised paragraph.

Figure 2. Beyond a read aloud: talking, thinking, and writing about literature.

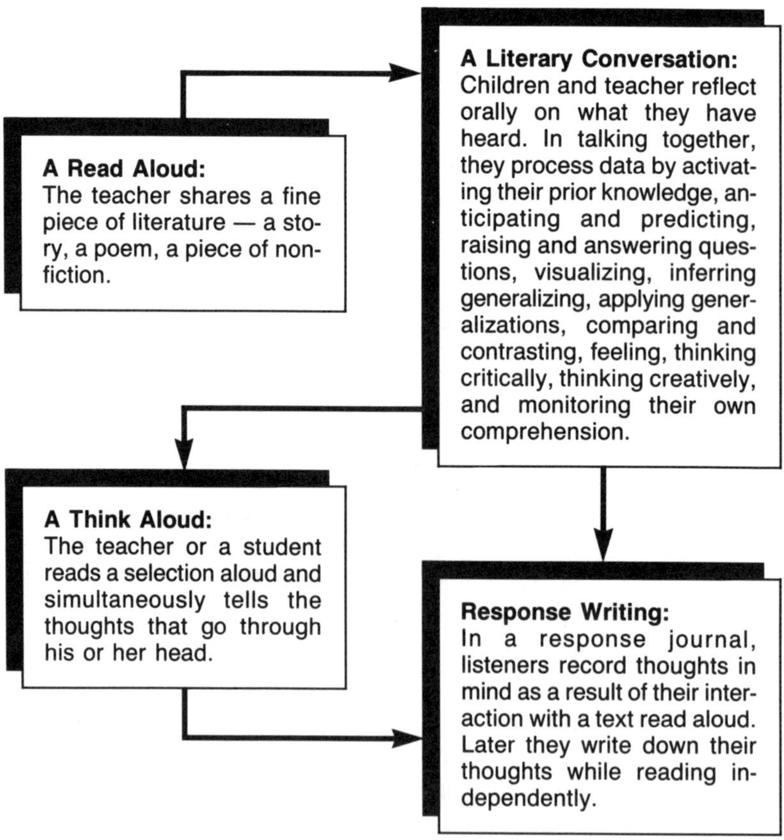

Independently, students write another paragraph expressing their opinion of Lazy Mazie, the second major character in the book. To guide their thinking and writing, students use the same reflective questions: "Do I like the character? Why? Why not?"

When students have finished writing their response paragraphs, they share and talk about them, which provides further opportunity for reflective thinking. Sharing their paragraphs also provides an opportunity for the young authors to find out what other listeners liked about what they wrote.

Summary

In this chapter, we have explained listening and reading as closely related reflective processes. Good listeners and readers make a variety of meanings as they interact with texts they are receiving. Before beginning, they prepare by activating their prior knowledge, anticipating and predicting, inferring, raising questions, and setting a purpose. While they listen and read, they make connections between what they already know and what they are receiving by visualizing, inferring, generalizing, applying generalizations, comparing, identifying other examples, organizing, and interpreting their own feelings. They extend the author's ideas by thinking critically and creatively. Throughout, they monitor their understanding. After they listen and read, they pursue ideas as the situation demands.

Teachers need to provide many opportunities for students at every level to reflect in these ways. These opportunities for reflection include but are not limited to read alouds, literary conversations, think alouds, and response writing. Using these instructional approaches, teachers are connecting listening with reading; they are using oral language to model and to teach the kind of reflective thinking that is at the heart of both listening and reading.

In the three chapters that follow, you will read about teachers who are using these approaches to engage students in reflecting on literature. In Chapter 2, you will meet Ms. O'Dell and her kindergartners and watch them as they go beyond a read aloud to think, talk, and write in response to some picture storybooks. In Chapter 3, you will meet Mr. Wexler and his seventh-graders and watch them interact with a series of poems. In Chapter 4, you will meet Mr. Lugo and his fourth-graders and watch them make meaning with two nonfiction pieces. In each instance, you will see a teacher using a read aloud and related oral language activity to help children acquire reflective-thinking strategies important in both listening to and reading fine literature.

References

Beyer, Barry. *Developing a Thinking Skills Program*. Boston: Allyn & Bacon, 1988.

Bosma, Bette. "The Nature of Critical Thinking: Its Base and Boundary." Paper presented at a meeting of the National Council of Teachers of English, Los Angeles, November 1987.

Bromley, Karen. *Webbing with Literature: Creating Story Maps with Children's Books*. Boston: Allyn & Bacon, 1991.

Corson, David. *Oral Language Across the Curriculum*. Clevedon, England: Multilingual Matters, 1987.

Cox, Carole, and Many, Joyce. "Toward an Understanding of the Aesthetic Response to Literature." *Language Arts* 69 (January 1992): 28-33.

Genishi, Celia; McCarrier, Andrea; and Nussbaum, Nancy. "Research Currents: Dialogue as a Context for Teaching and Learning." *Language Arts* 65 (February 1988): 182-91.

Hall, Lawrence. "The Wages of Syntax: Dictionary Reveals English's Bright Past, Potentially Dark Future." *Newark Star Ledger*, 23 May 1990, p. 23.

Hancock, Marjorie. "Literature Response Journals: Insights Beyond the Printed Page." *Language Arts* 69 (January 1992): 36-42.

Hennings, Dorothy Grant. *Communication in Action: Teaching the Language Arts*. 4th ed. Boston: Houghton Mifflin, 1990.

Kelly, Patricia. "Guiding Young Students' Response to Literature." *Reading Teacher* 43 (March 1990): 464-70.

Kemmel, Margaret Mary, and Segel, Elizabeth. *For Reading Out Loud!* New York: Delacorte, 1988.

Konigsburg, E.L. *From the Mixed-Up Files of Mrs. Basil E. Frankweiler*. New York: Atheneum, 1972.

Lipman, Matthew. "Critical Thinking: What Can It Be?" *Educational Leadership* 46 (September 1988): 39.

Moffett, James. "Reading and Writing as Meditation." *Language Arts* 60 (March 1983): 315-17.

Pearson, P. David, and Johnson, Dale. *Teaching Reading Comprehension*. New York: Holt, Rinehart and Winston, 1978.

Robinson, Francis. *Effective Study*. New York: Harper & Row, 1961.

Rosenblatt, Louise. *The Reader, the Text, the Poem*. Carbondale: Southern Illinois University Press, 1978.

Rumelhart, David. "Understanding Understanding." In *Understanding Reading Comprehension*, edited by James Flood. Newark, Del.: International Reading Association, 1984.

Shuy, Roger. "Research Currents: Dialogue as the Heart of Learning." *Language Arts* 64 (December 1987): 890-97.

Sinatra, Richard C. *Visual Literacy Connections to Thinking, Reading, and Writing*. Springfield, Ill.: Charles C. Thomas, 1986.
Smith, Frank. "The Unspeakable Habit." *Language Arts* 59 (September 1982): 551-52.
Stauffer, Russell. *The Language Experience Approach to the Teaching of Reading*. 2nd ed. New York: Harper & Row, 1980.
Tierney, Robert. "Redefining Reading Comprehension." *Educational Leadership* 47 (March 1990): 37-42.
Trelease, Jim. "Jim Trelease Speaks on Reading Aloud." *The Reading Teacher* 43 (December 1989). a
Trelease, Jim. *The New Read Aloud Handbook*. New York: Penguin, 1989. b
Vygotsky, Lev. *Thought and Language*. Cambridge, Mass.: MIT Press, 1986.
Wells, Gordon. *The Meaning Makers*. Portsmouth, N.H.: Heinemann, 1986.

2

A SHARED STORY EXPERIENCE:

REFLECTIVE LISTENING IN KINDERGARTEN

Stories are ideal for engaging very young children in thinking reflectively. Fine stories typically have a clear structure that makes them easy to follow. They grab the imagination; they engage feelings. There is much pleasure to be had in listening to and playing with a good story. As Don Holdaway (1989) explains, "Most children would agree that listening to stories is a most enjoyable activity, especially during the early years of schooling. Most teachers do read to their children and they, too, enjoy the experience."

In this chapter you will read about a group of kindergartners and their attempt to make meaning as they listen to and talk about a picture storybook. As you meet these children and their teacher, Ms. O'Dell, consider the objectives this teacher has in mind, the strategies she uses to achieve her objectives, and the assumptions she holds about teaching young children to listen and read.

Wandering with Three Ducks

It was a lovely spring morning – a perfect morning for thinking about farms, animals, and the out-of-doors. And so as the kindergartners came into their classroom, Ms. O'Dell settled herself on the "author's hassock" and gathered the children around her on the "communication rug." She asked the youngsters to talk about their walks to school that morning – things they had done, things they had noticed, things they had felt. With this introduction based on personal experience, Ms. O'Dell announced, "Today I am going to read to you one of my favorite stories." She displayed the front cover of a picture storybook and asked the children to describe what they saw. The children pointed to and together counted three ducks. The teacher then asked these questions:

Who do you think are going to be the main characters in this story? How many ducks are going to be in the story? (anticipating and predicting)
Are the ducks moving slowly or quickly? Why do you think that? (inferring to prepare students to interpret the word, *wandering*)
Where do ducks generally live? (activating prior knowledge)
Where do these ducks live – in the city or in the country? How do you know? (inferring from cover clues)
If the ducks live in the country, whom do you think they might meet? What do you think could happen to them? (anticipating and predicting)

Ms. O'Dell drew the students' attention to the title words. Pointing to the four words, she read them aloud, running her finger from left to right as she read, *Three Ducks Went Wandering*. Then repointing, she asked the youngsters to read the title words together. The children read the title words several times, with different children volunteering to point at the words. The teacher asked, "Were we right when we predicted that this story is about three ducks?" and the children called out, "Yes."

Ms. O'Dell then asked: "Who can show me the meaning of the word *wandering* by getting up and wandering about the classroom?" Three youngsters joined hands; and, pretending they were the story ducks, they pantomimed the meaning of wandering. Several other children joined the duck line and wandered, too. Working with other words on the cover, specifically the word, *by*, Ms. O'Dell re-read the title and read the smaller-sized words, *by Ron Roy*, *pictures by Paul Galdone*. She invited the children to re-read the words as she pointed. She explained to them that "by Ron Roy" means Mr. Roy had written the story just as they wrote stories in their class during writing workshop, and that "pictures by Paul Galdone" meant Mr. Galdone had painted the picture on the cover and those in the book.

Turning the cover over, Ms. O'Dell displayed the back side with a picture of a fox. She asked:

Who is going to be another character in this story? What do you think the fox is thinking in this picture? (anticipating and predicting)

What do you guess is going to happen in the story? Do you think the story will be exciting? Why? (anticipating and predicting)

Turning to the title page, Ms. O'Dell encouraged the kindergartners to read along as she pointed to title words and words about the author and illustrator. Holding up the title page that showed Mother Duck, she questioned:

Who may be another character in this story? (anticipating and predicting)

Where are the little ducks going to wander? (anticipating and predicting)

Why do you think the three ducks went wandering? (inferring a reason)

Turning to the opening spread that depicts a farm, Ms. O'Dell engaged the students in a brief discussion of what they already knew about a farm (activating prior knowledge). She asked the students to identify the other farm animals shown. Then she explained, "Girls and boys, before I read a story, I always like to think about the pictures on the cover, the title page, and the opening spread. I like to do what we just did – guess what may happen in the story before beginning to read" (demonstrating a self-monitoring behavior).

The First Day: Sharing the Story

Ms. O'Dell announced, "Now let's sit back and enjoy this story. Listen to see if your predictions about what is going to happen in the story are right." The teacher read aloud the first page, holding the book so the children could see the pictures. Reading the last sentence of the page, "They waddled past the barn and across the field, RIGHT IN FRONT OF . . ." she asked the children to repeat with her the big words at the end of the page, "RIGHT IN FRONT OF." The children enthusiastically joined in, and some went on to finish the sentence by calling out, "a fox!" Ms. O'Dell turned the page and showed the next picture – a picture of a bull. The children changed their predictions and chorused out, "a big cow." The teacher read, "A BIG, ANGRY BULL!"

She read the page and turned to the next to show a picture of the bull chasing the ducks. "What is going to happen to the ducks? What is going to happen to the bull?" she asked the listening children. The children eagerly predicted what would happen and sat back as the teacher read the next pages and showed the pictures. The youngsters laughed when they saw the picture of the bull laid flat by a crash into a fence. One youngster spontaneously exclaimed, "He deserved that."

Following a similar pattern of instruction based on Russell Stauffer's Directed Listening-Thinking Activity, the teacher orally shared the successive events in the story, pausing briefly for the children to predict whom the ducks would meet and what was going to happen next. She stopped very briefly before reading the last page to give the children time to anticipate the ending of the story.

Finishing the story, Ms. O'Dell drew the children's attention to the phrase, *right in front of*, which she had printed on the chalkboard. Pointing at it from left to right, she had the children chorus it together.

Then she asked, "What part of the story was the most fun? What part or picture did you like best?" In response, the children came forward to show their favorite pages, to tell or role play what happened at that point in the story, and to tell why they liked that part. Ms. O'Dell encouraged the children to give reasons to support their opinions by simply asking, "Why did you like that part?"

Continuing with the after-listening talk-out, Ms. O'Dell asked, "Think about another day when the three ducks went wandering. Whom could they walk right in front of?" Saying the last four words, Ms. O'Dell pointed to them on the board. Children called out their ideas (horses, owls, more ducklings, spiders), and some youngsters told what they thought would happen to the ducks. Ms. O'Dell wrote the names of the animals that the children suggested on a chart.

After sharing the story, the children went back to their individual work stations. They knew that they could write their own stories about what happened on other days when the three ducklings went wandering. They also knew that if they wished to re-read *Three Ducks Went Wandering*, they would find it on the reading table. Available on the reading carousel were other easy picture storybooks in paperback that children could read to themselves by predicting from the pictures and from the few words they could recognize.

The Second Day: Sharing, Re-reading, and Reflecting

The next afternoon, Ms. O'Dell again gathered her kindergartners on the communication rug. She asked if anyone would like to share a story he or she had written in response to yesterday's story. Several eagerly volunteered. These girls and boys took turns sitting on the author's hassock, displaying their story, and reading it to the listening group, much as their teacher had displayed and shared *Three Ducks Went Wandering*. The others listened so that they could retell the "author's" story (what Ms. O'Dell called receiving the story) and so that they could tell what they liked about it (what Ms. O'Dell called celebrating the story).

Then Ms. O'Dell picked up *Three Ducks Went Wandering*. Pointing to the title, author, and illustrator, she nodded at the children in a way that meant "read along with me." The kindergartners happily joined in to chorus the title, author, and illustrator. They also chorused the key story phrase, *right in front of*, that Ms. O'Dell had printed on the chalkboard and to which she pointed as they chorused the phrase together. With that, Ms. O'Dell proceeded to re-read the entire story, encouraging the youngsters to join in whenever they could anticipate what was coming and especially to contribute the phrase, "right in front of," when it was appropriate. Before beginning she had the children chorus that phrase several times as youngsters took turns pointing to it on the board.

When the children had re-read the story from beginning to end, the teacher pulled an easel with chart paper onto the communication rug and wrote the word, "Where?" She read the word and children joined in re-reading it. "Where did this story take place?" she questioned. Students together chorused the answer – on a farm. Ms. O'Dell wrote the words "on a farm" on the chart. Then she wrote the word, "When?" on the chart and asked the children if they remembered when the story took place. To help them answer, she re-read the first line of the story that starts, "One fine day." One youngster who could print letters copied this phrase from the book onto the chart. Ms. O'Dell then wrote the word, "Who?" on the chart. She asked the children who were the characters in the story. Several youngsters turned the pages of the book and dictated characters based on the pictures as Ms. O'Dell recorded the names on the chart. She also wrote the words, "What happened?" on the chart, read the words aloud pointing from left to right, and asked the children to retell what happened. To help them remember the order of events, several youngsters again turned the pages of the book. Ms. O'Dell wrote down the sentences that the children dictated to summarize what happened.

Ms. O'Dell invited the children to read and re-read their literature-based, language-experience chart. During the first re-reading, she pointed at the words, moving her hand from left to right as the children read. On successive readings, children volunteered to lead the reading by pointing.

The Third Day: Visualizing Story Relationships

The next day when the kindergartners gathered on the communication rug, they started by reading their literature-based, language-experience chart from the previous afternoon. The teacher had posted an outline map of the story on a second easel (see Figure 3). She asked the youngsters, "What animals could I draw in the barnyard? Who was there when the story started?" The children told about the three ducklings and the mother duck. The teacher quickly sketched the ducks there. Then using the story map, she retold the first segment of *Three Ducks Went Wandering* and moved her finger from the barnyard to the first X on the map. She asked the youngsters, "What animal did the ducks wander right in front of? What animal could I draw next at the first X?" The youngsters suggested the bull.

Ms. O'Dell asked one child to come up and point out the way the ducks went next and to suggest what animals they could draw at the next X – what animals the ducks wandered in front of. Children

Figure 3. A story map for the book, *Three Ducks Went Wandering*.

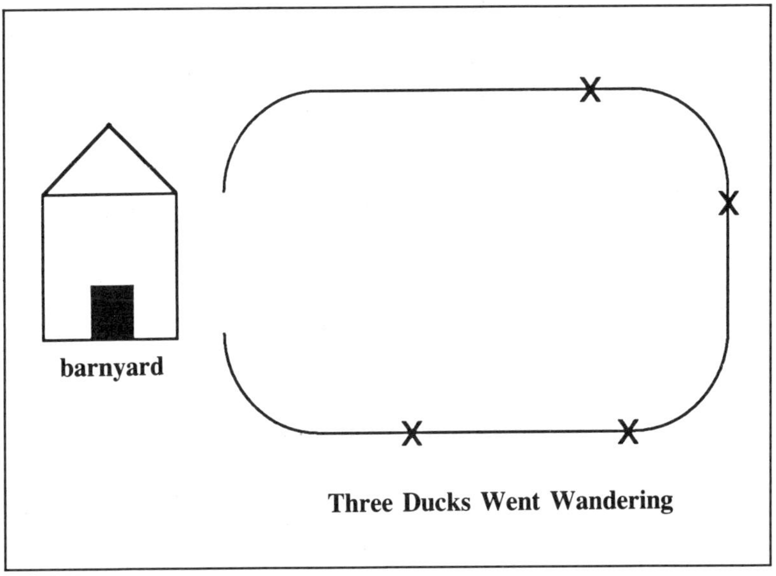

took turns coming forward to retell the story in their own words and to suggest the animal to draw next. Having retold the story together, the children each received a blank copy of the story map to take back to their work tables. They were to add drawings to the map that would help them picture what happened in the story. They could add any words or letters from words that they knew, such as "right in front of."

The kindergartners made their drawings and colored them. When they had finished, they used their maps to retell the story to a friend and then posted them on a bulletin board.

The Fourth Day: Making Contact with Feelings

The next morning as the children listened again to the story of the three ducklings, each one held a large piece of paper on which he or she had drawn a big exclamation mark. As the teacher read a sentence that the children felt showed lots of excitement, they held up their exclamation marks and joined in the re-reading, showing the excitement with their voices. Since the children now were very familiar with this story, most of them read right along with the teacher.

When Ms. O'Dell had finished the story, she asked some questions that helped the children clarify feelings. She asked:

How did the ducks feel when they started wandering? (inferring feelings) What were they probably saying to themselves? (thinking creatively)

Did the bull see the ducks? How do you know? (inferring) How did the bull feel? (inferring feelings) What was the bull probably saying to himself at this point? (thinking creatively)

Did the ducks see the bull? How do you know? (inferring) What were the ducks probably saying to themselves at this point? (thinking creatively)

How did the bull feel when he crashed into the fence? (inferring feelings) What did the bull probably say to himself at this point? (thinking creatively)

How did the foxes feel when they saw the ducks? How do you know? (inferring feelings) How do you think they felt when the ducks swam away? (inferring feelings) What did the foxes probably say to themselves at this point? What did the ducks say to themselves as they swam away? (thinking creatively)

Ms. O'Dell asked similar questions for the remaining events in the story – questions that forced the youngsters to think about the feelings and thoughts of the story characters. The students played the roles of the story characters and spoke the characters' thoughts. Then the teacher explained that when she reads a story, she generally thinks about what the characters might have been feeling and saying to themselves. She said, "You try to do this, too, when you listen to me read a story to you."

In seeking closure to the lesson, Ms. O'Dell helped the children to reflect on the main point of the story. She asked, "How did the ducks feel when they started wandering? How did they feel when they got home to their mother?" She guided the children to verbalize the idea that it feels good to go away from home but it feels even better to return home, that it is fun to explore but there is no place like home. She explained to the children that stories sometimes teach a lesson and that, when she reads a story, she tries to figure out that lesson, just as they had done together with *Three Ducks Went Wandering*.

The Fifth Day: Comparing and Contrasting

The next time the children gathered on the communication rug, Ms. O'Dell had a big-book version of *Rosie's Walk* by Pat Hutchins posted on the easel. The children reflected on the cover art, the title, and the author before she shared the book with them. The children also predicted what they thought might happen in this story.

Ms. O'Dell then read the story aloud, pointing to the words with a clear-plastic ruler. Having read the story once, she invited the children to retell the story, using the enlarged pictures of the big book as a guide. Then she asked them to role play the thoughts of the fox and Rosie. The children took turns telling what each of the story characters was thinking on each page of the story.

Having played the roles in the story, the students told what parts of it they liked best. Most of the kindergartners especially liked the page in which the swarm of bees chased the fox.

At that point, Ms. O'Dell asked the children to think about the two stories, *Rosie's Walk* and *Three Ducks Went Wandering*. "How were the stories the same?" she asked. To help the students reflect, she prompted, "Where did both stories take place? What kind of day was it? How did both stories begin? What did the main characters do in both stories? How did both stories end?" With these kinds of prompts, the children were able to offer simple comparisons. Ms. O'Dell then helped them to organize a chart of comparisons based on what they had said.

When the children had finished dictating their story-comparison chart, Ms. O'Dell read it while pointing to the words. Volunteers came forward to re-read segments of the chart, also pointing as they read.

Ms. O'Dell suggested to the children that when they returned to their work stations, they might want to write their own story about an animal who went for a walk that was like *Three Ducks Went Wandering* and *Rosie's Walk*. She suggested that they pick a character other than a hen or ducks. She asked, "What would make a good story character to write about?" Children suggested other barnyard animals, such as a sheep, a horse, a cat, a dog, a pig, a rooster. Ms. O'Dell reminded the children that in writing they could use any combination of drawings, lines, letters, numbers, and words they wanted. The idea was to get their story down so that they could later share it from the author's hassock.

The Teacher's Objectives and Strategies

What were Ms. O'Dell's objectives in planning and teaching this five-day lesson series with the stories *Three Ducks Went Wandering* and *Rosie's Walk*? What did she hope the children would learn?

Ms. O'Dell's primary objective was that the young children enjoy making meaning with a story. She hoped to instill in her children a love of books and of reading so that they would ask her to share more books as well as seek out books to read on their own.

In addition, Ms. O'Dell hoped the youngsters would refine their ability to reflect on stories and their understanding of story structure, design, and mood. More specifically, she wanted them to use their emerging understanding of key story elements and aspects of story design and mood as a framework for activating related knowledge before listening, predicting before and while listening, inferring, visualizing, organizing story data as a chart, perceiving similarities between two stories, identifying story feelings and lessons, expressing opinions and reasons for their opinions, and creating a story with elements similar to those in the stories they had heard.

Ms. O'Dell knew that these understandings about stories and these ways of reflecting on them are not mastered in one sitting, especially by very young children. For this reason, she did not state her objectives as "By the end of the lesson, the students will be able to . . ." She thought instead, "Through this lesson, the students will refine their ability to . . ."

How did Ms. O'Dell work toward these fundamental objectives? As you have seen, she used a variety of strategies:

A Story-Based Conversation. Ms. O'Dell began by reading a regular-sized paperback book. She wanted to introduce children to books similar to the kind they would read independently. Additionally, she shared a big book in which the print and the pictures can be seen by listeners in a group. Using the big book, she modeled how people read from top to bottom and from left to right. She pointed to the words as she read to show this progression and also to help children begin to connect spoken thoughts with words on paper.

Later, when she re-read the big book with the children, she would invite students to join in the reading and to take turns pointing at the words. She did this because she knew that some of the kindergartners had not fully developed the concept of a word. They had trouble connecting spoken words with individual words on paper and needed practice making the connection as they listened to and read an actual story.

Sharing easy picture books in a regular or an enlarged version provides a meaningful context for encouraging young children to reflect, especially to activate prior knowledge, to anticipate and predict, and to infer before reading. Guided by their teacher's questions, young children can talk about the pictures on the cover, title page, and opening spread before listening to the story and can make predictions and inferences about the story based on the picture clues. When the teacher shares two or more stories, as Ms. O'Dell did, students can also reflect on similarities between the stories. Learning to reflect in this natural way, youngsters simultaneously are learning basic components of story structure and are using them as a framework to guide their listening.

As follow-up to a story read aloud, the teacher can help students chart the key elements of the story. Ms. O'Dell used a modification of the language-experience approach (Stauffer 1969). When the children had experienced *Three Ducks Went Wandering*, she had them talk about essential elements of the story – where, when, who, and what happened. As children told about these elements, she recorded their words as a chart. She did the same as the children made simple comparisons of the two stories they had heard.

Dictating and then reading and re-reading their charts, children are developing basic reading skills – top-to-bottom progression, left-to-right progression, concept of word, and sight word vocabulary.

They are building these skills based on content that is meaningful to them. In addition, when charts are tabular and contain points suggested by children, the students are learning a way of reflecting that is useful for both listening and reading – organizing to highlight relationships.

Stories also have a design, a pattern of action through which the plot develops. An understanding of these designs can increase comprehension as children listen to a story. Listeners use their general understanding of the ways in which stories develop to predict what will happen next in a particular story. This keeps them actively involved as they listen.

Ms. O'Dell shared a repetitive story. Stories in which words, phrases, sentences, or events repeat are excellent devices for encouraging children to join in while listening. Listening to a repetitive story for the first time, children can guess words and read them right along with their teacher. Stories in which events recur each time with a slightly different twist also encourage prediction. Picking up the repetitive pattern, young listeners are able to anticipate where a story is going and how it will end.

Mapping a story helps children to visualize the design of a story and to organize their thinking about it. Talking and reflecting together, young children can map a circular story by drawing a series of pictures, each relating to a successive event in the story. Figure 3 on page 33 is an example of this kind of simple map. When stories are both circular and repetitive, children who have used a simple map can expand it to clarify the repetitive components.

The story map that these youngsters generated provided them with a strategy to highlight relationships. Story maps are good for clarifying sequence. They help young children to develop the concept of *first*, *second*, *then*, *next*, and *finally*. Youngsters must use these sequence words when they talk about the story as they map it. They must use them again as they retell the story based on their map.

Stories also have a mood, and that mood may fluctuate. Story characters feel happy or elated at some points in the story; they feel sad or depressed at others. Children can focus on feelings as they listen to a re-reading of a story and can talk about the characters' feelings. Very young children also can visually plot the rise and fall of feelings in a story by drawing happy and sad faces. When a character feels happy in a story, they draw a happy face on a chart; when that character feels sad, they draw a sad face.

Older children can graph the mood changes. They plot the words *happy*, *in-between*, and *sad* (or comparable words) on the y-axis, and *story beginning*, *story middle*, and *story end* on the x-axis. This kind of activity helps children visualize story relationships. It also provides students with a way to reflect while and after listening or reading.

Not only do fine stories have a structure, a design, and a mood, most also develop around a main idea, or theme, which must be inferred. Just as Ms. O'Dell did, the teacher may have to guide young children in figuring out the meaning of the story by asking a series of focused questions. This is a good way to conclude a story-based conversation – by encouraging children to talk about the lesson the story is teaching.

Most of the activities Ms. O'Dell initiated were oral; children were involved primarily as listeners and speakers. However, Ms. O'Dell wanted the children to begin to apply their growing reflective-thinking abilities not only as they listened but also as they read independently. That was the reason why, after reading the book aloud, Ms. O'Dell placed *Three Ducks Went Wandering* at the reading-center table and why she displayed other books on a reading carousel. Working from the pictures and the words that they could figure out, students could re-read the shared book to themselves or a friend or could select another book that interested them. In doing this, Ms. O'Dell was making the listening-reading connection.

Oral Vocabulary Play. Word knowledge plays a crucial role in listening and reading comprehension as well as in speaking and writing. As Devine (1986) explains, "Children, adolescents, and young adults cannot begin to comprehend unless they have meanings held in memory for such words as *fell, hurt, knee, be, question*, or *log*."

Although word knowledge is held in memory, children do not build this knowledge through memorization or by reading a definition in a dictionary. Words are labels for concepts, and "One of the axioms of instruction for concept development is that there is no substitute for direct experience" (Pearson and Johnson 1978). Children most readily acquire a concept of a zebra by seeing one. They learn best what an airplane is by flying in one.

But, as Pearson and Johnson caution, "The realities of classroom instruction make it impossible to rely on direct experience as the major vehicle for concept development." Instead, the way to proceed is to help children build concepts by "relating the new to the known." That was what Ms. O'Dell was doing as she and her students played with the words, *wandering*, *by*, and *right in front of*.

Ms. O'Dell used pantomime to involve her kindergartners directly in the words of the story. *Wandering* is a long word for kindergartners; but to get the point of the story, they must know that word. And so the teacher used the word orally before sharing the story and involved the children physically in its meaning; she had the children get up and wander. Ms. O'Dell also worked with the word *by*, relating its use on the cover to an act the youngsters had performed themselves, writing and illustrating stories. And she highlighted one phrase from the story, *right in front of,* so that the children would add the words in the phrase to their sight word vocabularies.

Reflective Writing. Writing is a way to make ideas stand still so that they can be modified and expanded. To help children learn to reflect as part of listening and reading, teachers must make the writing connection. This means that children write before, while, and after they listen and read, generally on topics they themselves select. Writing becomes an integral part of responding to literature.

Young children can respond to a story by composing sentences and short paragraphs in which they:

- predict what will happen in a story based on a preliminary survey of pictures and cover clues;
- retell the story in sequence;
- describe a story site after visualizing that site;
- describe a particular character after they have visualized him or her;
- ask a story character some questions;
- explain why a particular character in the story acted the way he or she did;
- tell how two characters are the same, how they differ;
- describe a time when they felt the same as a story character or did something just like a story character did;
- explain what they would have done at a particular point in the story if they had been a story character;
- tell which of two characters they like better and tell why they feel as they do;
- tell whether they like the story and give their reasons;
- create another adventure about the same character or characters;
- create another story set in the same place or at the same time;

- create another story with the same theme or main point;
- explain how one story is similar to another or how one story differs from a second;
- tell which story of two they prefer and give their reasons.

In responding to a story in these ways, children are making connections by visualizing, inferring, generalizing, comparing, and feeling. They also are extending story content by thinking critically and creatively about it.

Ms. O'Dell used a combination of specific strategies to encourage her kindergartners to write in response to a story. One strategy she used was invented spelling. Children in Ms. O'Dell's class used a combination of drawings, letters, numbers, and words – whatever means at their command – to communicate their ideas on paper. Emphasis was on the process of getting ideas down, not on producing a "perfect" end product.

Young children who write with invented spellings can put their ideas on paper from the first day of school. They do not have to learn to read before they can write, nor do they have to know all the letters of the alphabet before becoming writers (Graves 1983; Calkins 1986). Because they live in a print-rich world, children learn to write by writing naturally to communicate their ideas.

A second strategy Ms. O'Dell emphasized was rehearsing before writing. Before they wrote stories of their own, children listened to stories and talked about them. They brainstormed possible characters for stories; they composed, modeling their stories after ones heard or read; and they talked as they composed. Ms. O'Dell made conversing an integral part of the writing process as children got ready to write. By doing this, she demonstrated the avenues for reflection that youngsters could explore in their own writing.

Ms. O'Dell also relied on collaborative writing. Together the teacher and children retold the story they had heard; together they created a chart with story highlights. A number of researchers (Morrow 1985; Gambrell, Pfeiffer, and Wilson 1985; Gambrell, Koskinen, and Kapinus 1985) suggest that it is important for children to retell key story elements and happenings after listening and reading. Charts can be used to help children retell a story in their own words.

Ms. O'Dell also encouraged her youngsters to share what they had written. She recognized them as authors and asked them to read what they had written in the same manner as she had read the books of published authors – sitting on the author's hassock and reading to their classmates, who reflect on their writing by retelling and by celebrating, that is, saying what they liked about the story.

Modeling. Young children learn from models. Youngsters' first words are those they have heard used by their caregivers. They pattern their early attempts to tie shoelaces after the model demonstrated by their parents. Models are important in learning.

As she taught, Ms. O'Dell actively modeled ways of reflecting in listening and in interacting with written text. The models she used were of three kinds. First, she talked the children step by step through reflective activities before, during, and after they listened to a story. In raising questions, in encouraging them to think about the thoughts that the story animals had in mind, in engaging the children in mapping the story, she was modeling for the children the way to make meaning in listening, the way to proceed when they listen and when they read on their own. In this respect, she was teaching youngsters reflective strategies; she was providing them with a model of how to do it.

Second, at times Ms. O'Dell told the children what she thought about as she reflected on a story. She explained to them that she thought about what the characters might have been feeling and thinking; and she said, "You try to do this, too, when you listen to me read a story to you." In doing this, she was using her own behavior as a model for them to follow.

Third, she encouraged students to create their own stories modeled after the stories they had heard. Writing about further adventures of the ducklings or about other animals who went wandering, young authors begin to use the kinds of structures that make fine stories. They include in their stories a time and a place; they have their characters meet and overcome danger. Through listening to stories, and especially by predicting continuously while listening, children are learning to think as writers do.

Assumptions About Language Arts Instruction

Ms. O'Dell's lesson sequence provides clues to what she holds important in teaching young children to listen. Quite clearly, this teacher believes in a literature-based approach to the language arts. She believes that through listening to and reflecting on stories, young children develop as skillful users and pursuers of their oral and written language. She knows that oral language activity organized around reading aloud provides opportunity for young children to develop and refine their ability not only to listen and to speak, but to read, to write, and to use language to think.

If an observer were to ask Ms. O'Dell what is the best way to teach young children to reflect on stories, she probably would generalize as follows:

Start with children listening to stories. Listening involves much more than hearing. To listen to a story with understanding, one must do more than perceive language sounds and differentiate among them. To listen with understanding, one must reflect on the ideas an author is communicating and construct meaning in response.

Engage children in talking about stories that they have heard. Literary conversation is an integral part of a read aloud, whether the teacher is sharing a story or whether children are sharing stories they have written. Talking before, during, and after listening models ways of thinking that children can use when they listen or read independently.

As a teacher involves young children in successive read alouds with a story, she can engage them in the ways of reflection that are at the heart of the listening process. Children listen and re-listen to real stories and reflect on them as part of a literary conversation. Ability to listen to a story with full comprehension is an acquired skill that depends to some extent on the listener's understanding of story structure, design, and mood.

As a teacher shares a story with young children, she can involve them in new vocabulary by providing direct experiences with the underlying concepts and by helping them make connections between the new and the known. A read-aloud/talk-out is a natural context for the conceptual development that is at the heart of building vocabulary.

A natural follow-up to a read-aloud/talk-out is response writing. Young children in kindergarten and primary grades are eager to write, especially when the teacher celebrates their early efforts. A natural follow-up to response writing is orally sharing children's stories. In writing and sharing, children apply their growing understanding of story structure, they learn what it means to be an author, and they begin to perceive themselves as writers.

Another natural follow-up to a read-aloud/talk-out is independent reading. Young children need not know the alphabet, have an extensive vocabulary, or have an in-depth understanding of letter-sound relationships to start reading. If reading is conceived as generating meaning, then young children can read on their own by predicting and inferring from pictorial clues. By reading, they create their original versions of a story; they become co-authors of it. In so doing, they begin to perceive themselves as readers – a perception very important in their emergence as literate human beings.

Listening to stories and conversing about them pave the way for reading stories with understanding. In reflecting before, during, and after listening, children are learning ways of processing text. These ways are similar whether a story is heard or read. That is one of the major advantages of story-based conversations. They help young children make the connection between reflective listening and reflective reading.

Children need to develop strategies for monitoring their own understanding as they listen and read. To help them, teachers should make explicit the ways they themselves reflect as they interact with a text before, during, and after they share a story.

To teach reflective thinking is to organize lessons that are based on meaningful content. There is little point in designing discrete, game-like activities or skill-building exercises that are divorced from ongoing classroom work and play. The curriculum offers a multitude of natural opportunities for students to reflect on worthwhile ideas.

References

Calkins, Lucy. *The Art of Teaching Writing*. Portsmouth, N.H.: Heinemann Educational Books, 1986.

Devine, Thomas. *Teaching Reading Comprehension: From Theory to Practice*. Boston: Allyn & Bacon, 1986.

Gambrell, Linda; Koskinen, Patricia; and Kapinus, Barbara. "A Comparison of Retelling and Questioning on Reading Comprehension." Paper presented at the National Reading Conference, San Diego, December 1985.

Gambrell, Linda; Pfeiffer, Warren; and Wilson, Robert. "The Effects of Retelling on Reading Comprehension." *Journal of Educational Research* 78 (July/August 1985): 216-20.

Gore, Kay. "DISKovery: Computers and Thinking Skills, The Hots Program." *Language Arts* 68 (February 1991): 151-58.

Graves, Donald. *Writing: Teachers and Children at Work*. Portsmouth, N.H.: Heinemann Educational Books, 1983.

Holdaway, Don. "Shared Book Experience: Teaching Reading Using Favorite Books." in *Whole Language: Beliefs and Practices, K-8*, edited by Gary Manning and Maryann Manning. Washington, D.C.: National Education Association, 1989.

Hutchins, Pat. *Rosie's Walk.* New York: Harper & Row, 1968.

Morrow, Leslie Mandel. "Retelling Stories: A Strategy for Improving Young Children's Comprehension of Story Structure and Oral Language Complexity." *The Elementary School Journal* 85 (1985): 647-61.

Pearson, P. David, and Johnson, Dale. *Teaching Reading Comprehension.* New York: Holt, Rinehart and Winston, 1978.

Roy, Ron. *Three Ducks Went Wandering.* Illustrated by Paul Galdone. New York: Clarion, 1980.

Stauffer, Russell. *Teaching Reading as a Thinking Process.* New York: Harper & Row, 1969.

3

A SHARED POETRY EXPERIENCE:

REFLECTIVE LISTENING IN JUNIOR HIGH

How do junior high school teachers help young people refine their ability to function as reflective listeners and readers? In upper grades, poetry is ideal for engaging young people in thinking reflectively. Poems typically have an underlying meaning that must be inferred and that causes listeners and readers to think about what they themselves believe and how they themselves feel. Also, poems are filled with sounds that make them a pleasure to hear. There is much joy to be had in listening and responding to a good poem.

In this chapter you will read about a group of seventh-grade students and their attempt to make meaning as they listen to, read, and respond to a series of related poems. As you meet these young people and their teacher, Brian Wexler, again consider the objectives the teacher had in mind, the strategies he was using to achieve his objectives, and the assumptions he held about teaching listening and reading to young people.

The First Day: Sharing Two Poems

When the students in Mr. Wexler's seventh-grade English class came into his classroom, he quickly checked the attendance and announced: "Today, we are going to play with poetry meanings. Through our activities, I am going to show you some of the things I think about as I listen to or read poetry so that you have a way of responding to poetry. You can also use some of these ways of thinking as you listen to or read fiction and nonfiction."

With that, Mr. Wexler announced that he was going to share a poem called "The Hippopotamus"; and he asked his students to picture, or visualize, a hippopotamus in their minds. He explained that when he reads the title of a poem, story, or selection that refers to something concrete, he always tries to picture that object in his mind's eye before actually reading the piece. Having painted their mental pictures, students called out words they would use to describe a hippopotamus. As students named words, their teacher recorded them as an interconnected web, as in Figure 4.

To trigger additional words, Mr. Wexler held up a picture of a hippo and asked students for words and phrases that came to mind. He also provided students with more words by reading aloud a series of sentences about a hippopotamus and having the students use context clues to predict the meanings of such technical terms as *aquatic, herbivore*, and *quadruped*.

Mr. Wexler then asked, "How many of you carry a positive view of a hippopotamus in your head? How many of you think negatively when you think about a hippopotamus? If you were writing about a hippo, what might you want to say about it? What big thought would you want to communicate?" Most students, though not all, recognized that they held a rather negative view of hippos; they suggested such ideas as: "Hippos are ugly animals; a hippo is not an animal to make friends with; and a hippo is a lot bigger and slower than most other animals." Mr. Wexler wrote these ideas around the edge of the hippo web he drew earlier. As he wrote, he explained: "To get myself ready to listen or read, I try to paint a picture in my head of the object or place or person about which I am going to listen or read. I also dredge up from my mind words that relate to the topic, and I ask myself – exactly as we just did, 'If I were going to write on this topic, what big idea would I want to communicate? Would I want to say something positive? Negative?' You may wish to do this before you listen to or read almost anything."

Mr. Wexler announced that he was going to read "The Hippopotamus" by Ogden Nash, a poet with whom the seventh-graders were not familiar. He explained that Nash often wrote poems that poke fun at the world, and that when he first reads a poem by Nash, he anticipates that it will be a bit humorous. He said, "Keep that in mind while you listen to 'The Hippopotamus.' Ask yourself, 'What is Nash

Figure 4. A prelistening web for generating ideas before reading the poem, *The Hippopotamus* by Ogden Nash.

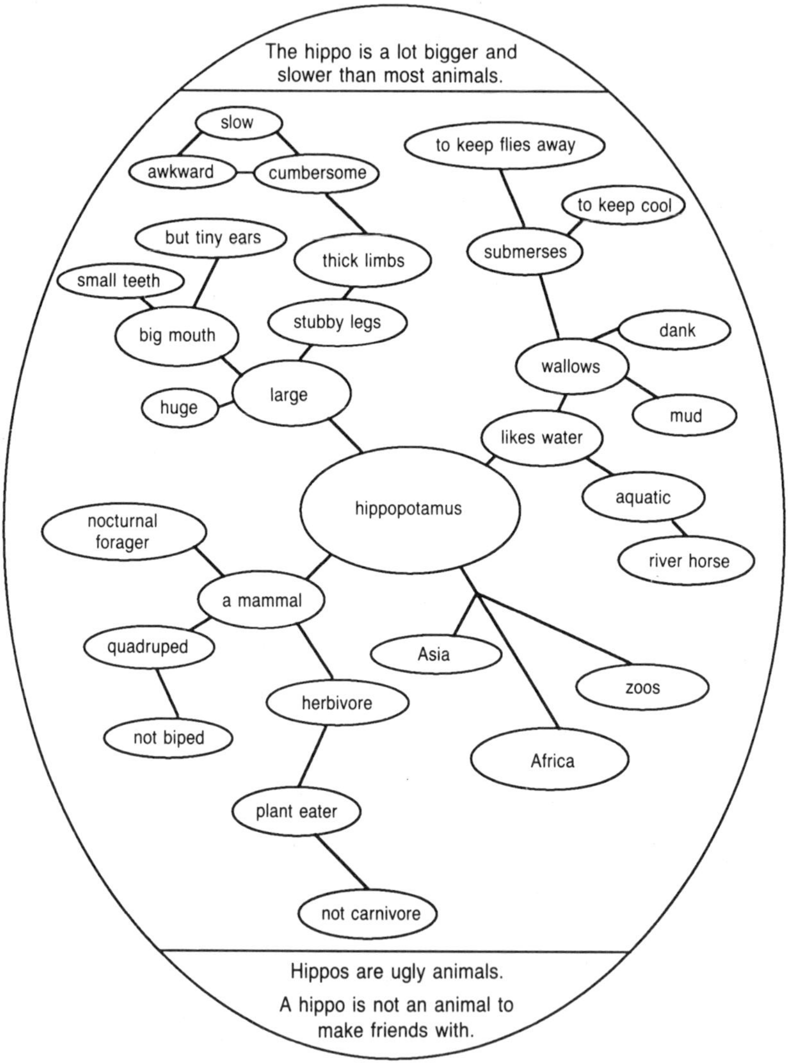

trying to say about a hippo?' " Then, using facial expressions and gestures to enhance meaning, Mr. Wexler recited the poem.

The Hippopotamus*

Behold the hippopotamus!
We laugh at how he looks to us,
And yet in moments dank and grim
I wonder how we look to him.

Peace, peace thou hippopotamus!
We really look all right to us,
As you no doubt delight the eye
Of other hippopotami.

Before reciting the poem a second time, Mr. Wexler told his students to think about what Nash was trying to say in the poem and to try to clarify the main idea. Students listened to the poem again and then talked about the main ideas they had identified. In the discussion, Mr. Wexler did not imply that there was one main idea; rather, he expected that each student would make meaning with the poem in a unique way.

One student proposed, "People laugh at the hippo."

A second added, "But we look funny to the hippo."

A third began to generalize, "We all appear a bit different to others."

A fourth also generalized, "Everybody views the world through his or her own prejudices."

Mr. Wexler asked, "What evidence do we have from the poem to support these ideas?" Students mentioned such phrases as "We laugh at how he looks to us," and "You delight the eye of other hippopotami," to support the idea that people use their own perceptions to judge others.

With that, students joined in as their teacher recited the Nash poem twice more. As they joined in, they thought about the tone Nash was communicating and tried to use their voices, gestures, and facial expressions to communicate that tone.

---

*From *Verses from 1929 On* by Ogden Nash, copyright 1935 by Ogden Nash. First appeared in *The Saturday Evening Post*. Copyright outside North America, © 1959 by Ogden Nash. Reprinted by permission of Curtis Brown, Ltd.

After reciting the poem, the seventh-graders and their teacher talked about satire and Nash's use of personification to help communicate his point. Then they read the poem to themselves from a transparency their teacher flashed on the screen. In reading, they studied the punctuation to see what clues Nash had supplied to assist them in their oral interpretation. Then from memory, following their teacher's lips, the students orally recited the poem, using their voices to communicate the humor and to reflect the punctuation marks.

When the class had recited the poem several times, Mr. Wexler asked if there was any word that was new to them. When students identified "dank" as an unfamiliar word, Mr. Wexler asked if not knowing the word interfered with their enjoying the poem and if they could predict what "dank" meant based on its use. The students checked a dictionary and expressed surprise that "dank" means damp. Most had predicted "low," "sad," or "unhappy." When Mr. Wexler asked why Nash used the uncommon "dank" rather than the more familiar "damp," students agreed that "dank" sounded more interesting and added to the overall effect of the poem, even though they had not known what it meant.

It had taken these seventh-graders about 20 minutes to listen to, recite, and reflect on "The Hippopotamus." With that introduction, Mr. Wexler asked his students to tell him how they had gone about making meaning with the poem. Students recalled that they had first thought about the title and anticipated what this author was going to say about the topic. They recalled that as they listened, they thought about the main idea Nash was trying to communicate. Having listened, they had specific clues from the poem that supported the main ideas they had proposed. They also recalled that they had recited the poem as a way of better understanding it.

Mr. Wexler asked, "When can we use such a meaning-making strategy?" Students suggested that they could use this meaning-making strategy not only when they were listening to and reading poems, but also when they were working with stories and expository texts.

Mr. Wexler then told the class that he was going to share another poem, "The Elephant, or the Force of Habit" by A.E. Housman. He asked students what they might do before hearing the poem. Students suggested visualizing an elephant and thinking about the meaning implied in the title. They raised the previewing questions: What comes to mind when we think of an elephant? What is meant by the phrase, "Force of Habit"? How do we react when we react out of habit? If we were writing about an elephant and the force of habit, what would we probably want to say?

Having pondered before listening, students listened as Mr. Wexler read the poem, using his arms to demonstrate physically the tail behind, the trunk in front.

The Elephant, or the Force of Habit*

A Tail behind, a trunk in front,
Complete the usual elephant.
The Tail in front, the trunk behind
Is what you very seldom find.

If you for specimens should hunt
With trunks behind and tails in front,
That hunt would occupy you long;
The force of habit is so strong.

Mr. Wexler recited the poem twice and then asked the students to join in as he recited it twice more. Then he projected a copy of it on the screen and asked students to read it to themselves.

Mr. Wexler urged students to think comparatively: How are the two poems similar? How are they different? He told the students that they were going to answer these questions in three-person teams and that they were also going to think about how the poems were similar to and different from a third poem, "Alligator/Crocodile" by Mary Ann Hoberman. In preparation, Mr. Wexler and the class constructed a chart to record their comparisons.

The student teams prepared to read the Hoberman poem by visualizing, brainstorming, and webbing, just as they had done for the other poems. Then they read the poem, first silently to themselves and then aloud in choral fashion to hear the sounds. The teams talked about the three poems and filled in their chart.

Using their completed charts to share their ideas, the teams came together as a class and discussed ways the poems were similar and

*From *My Brother, A.E. Housman* by Laurence Housman. Copyright 1937, 1938 by Laurence Housman, renewed 1964, 1965 by Lloyds Bank Ltd. Reprinted with permission of Charles Scribner's Sons, an imprint of Macmillan Publishing Company. Acknowledgement also made to the Estate of Laurence Housman and Jonathan Cape, publisher.

different. They generalized that the three poets were using their poems to say something fundamental about the world and that they were relying on satire to emphasize their ideas. Students identified which of the three poems they liked best and gave reasons to support their choices. Since students differed in their opinions, this generated considerable discussion.

The Second Day: Writing Poems

The next day Mr. Wexler asked students to sum up what they had done and what they had concluded during the prior class. To do this, the students referred to the charts they had compiled and the generalizations they had recorded in their notebooks. Then Mr. Wexler proposed, "Let us try to do some of the same things these poets did when they composed their poems. Let's create similar poems. I'll show you how you could begin."

With that, Mr. Wexler wrote the word "raccoon" on the board and asked students to brainstorm words that came to their minds when they visualized a raccoon. A student recorded the words in a word web on the board. The teacher then displayed a realistic hand puppet of a raccoon and asked for more words. To focus on a main idea to be expressed, he asked, "What fundamental idea about the world could we communicate using the raccoon as an example, as evidence to support the idea?" Students made suggestions that were recorded around the perimeter of the word web.

At that point, Mr. Wexler drew the students' attention to a list posted on the bulletin board. He explained that he had found it easier to compose when he started with a structure or pattern and expanded from there. The list presented a pattern for writing poems line by line:

- First line: the name of the object.
- Second line: adjectives to describe the object.
- Third line: "-ing" verb.
- Fourth line: "-ing" verb.
- Fifth line: "-ing" verb.
- Sixth line: a creative comparison.

Guided by the teacher, the class working as a whole composed a poem about a raccoon, including much revising to expand the lines to add more adjectives, adverbs, and prepositional phrases. The result was:

Midnight Bandit

Masked raccoon –
Wary, watchful
Waiting in the stillness and the darkness of the night,
Coming with a crash of cans,
Taking what *he* wants,
Doing what *he* wants –
A midnight bandit on the loose.

Having composed and revised together, the students read their poem together. They identified what they liked and did not like about their poem. They discussed the fact that their poem did not rhyme but still had the sound of poetry because of the rhythm and alliteration.

Mr. Wexler had posted some striking photographs of animals around the room. Now he explained to the students that the remainder of the class would be a writing workshop. During the writing workshop, students could:

- compose a poem about an animal that incorporated elements from the Nash, Housman, and Hoberman poems or from the class poem. They could do this on their own or in teams.
- write an informational paragraph about the hippo, drawing words and data from the word web. They also could do this on their own or in teams.
- write something that was in their heads that morning that they needed to say.
- edit or revise a composition of their choice from their writing portfolio – a piece they wanted to work on for publication.
- cooperate with another student to edit or revise a composition composed during a previous workshop.
- meet with the teacher for a pre-publication conference.
- cooperate with another student to search through classroom poetry anthologies for an animal poem that reminded them of those studied and prepare that poem for oral sharing with classmates.

At the end of the workshop, Mr. Wexler asked students who had composed or searched for animal poems to read their pieces to the class. Other students commented on what they felt the author was trying to communicate and on what they felt were good words and phrases that the author had used. In two instances, student authors indicated that they had had trouble with a particular line and asked for help in making the line better. Classmates offered suggestions.

To sum up, Mr. Wexler reminded the students that it is important for an author to have an idea in mind to communicate through his or her writing. As readers, students should actively search for the significant ideas being communicated. As writers – like Nash, Housman, and Hoberman – they should focus on an idea they want to get across to their audience and provide evidence to support that idea.

The Teacher's Objectives and Strategies

Mr. Wexler's primary objective in this two-day unit was that his students enjoy making meaning with poems. He hoped to instill in the students an appreciation of the sounds and imagery of poetry so that they would search for poems to read on their own and would select poetry writing as an option during future writing workshops.

In addition, Mr. Wexler hoped that the students would refine their understanding of style in writing. He wanted them to be able to recognize when an author is using satire to communicate some fundamental truth about the way the world works. He also wanted the students: 1) to prepare for listening and reading by visualizing, by activating related knowledge, and by predicting; 2) to use their voices, faces, and bodies to express meaning; 3) to identify a main idea while listening or reading and to support that idea with evidence; 4) to organize a data chart to clarify similarities and differences among poems; 5) to formulate opinions and support those opinions with facts; 6) to develop a main idea for composing; and 7) to enjoy sharing what they had written.

What has been described here is a read aloud with poetry. In the case of poetry, a read aloud takes on special dimensions. The read aloud begins with an oral sharing of the poem through recitation or reading by the teacher. Initially students do not see the text of the poem. Their first encounter with a poem is oral; they hear it and gradually join in while listening. Students chorus the poem over and over, each time varying their interpretation to heighten their comprehension and enjoyment of the piece. When they eventually read the poem and study its form, they bring to their interpretation an understanding based on their enjoyment of its sounds; they bring to their reading a "feel" for poetry that helps them reflect more deeply. In this way, young people gain ownership of a poem; they can repeat it from memory and are able to make meaning with it.

Mr. Wexler used a variety of strategies, including a focus unit, poetry sharing and chorusing, an in-depth poetry conversation, oral play with word meanings, cooperative learning, and a writing workshop. Let us consider each of these approaches, thinking especially about the way these strategies provide opportunities for students to reflect in response to literature.

Focus Units. Focus units are a sequence of activities based on several literary works that share a common element. Joy Moss (1984), a long-time advocate of teaching communication and reading skills through focus units, describes one for early primary youngsters in which the teacher selected a series of stories about bears to share orally with young students. During the unit, the youngsters listened to, thought about, talked about, wrote about, drew pictures about, and engaged in dramatic play about bears. You saw a focus unit in action at the kindergarten level in Chapter 2, where Ms. O'Dell, built a unit around two stories (*Three Ducks Went Wandering* and *Rosie's Walk*). She used those stories not because they shared a common topic but because they shared a common structure.

Focus units also have a place in the upper grades, as demonstrated by Mr. Wexler's concise unit based on a series of animal poems. In building a poetry focus unit, the teacher and students select several short poems that are easy to recite and that share a common element. The poems may be about the same topic (animals, machines, cities, a season of the year), make a similar point, be by the same author, have a similar structure, or make use of the same literary devices (satire, personification, metaphor, rhyme, alliteration, assonance). The focus unit also may include related stories and informational pieces. Unit activities, especially language-development activities, emerge out of transactions with the selections.

In the upper grades, an advantage of organizing around focus units rather than individual poems or stories is that there is considerable opportunity to encourage students to think in depth about the selections. Students are able to compare and contrast, to formulate opinions, to generalize, and to create. Students also are able to apply thinking strategies they have learned in the context of one selection to their interpretation of related selections.

Poetry anthologies and collections of works by one author are helpful in organizing poetry focus units. Some anthologies focus on a single topic and contain short poems that are perfect for reciting, joining in while listening, and writing after listening.

Sharing Poetry and Chorusing. Mr. Wexler did not introduce his students to the first poem, "The Hippopotamus," by assigning them to read it by themselves. Rather, he recited it several times and then asked the students to listen to and join in on the words they remembered. When his students interpreted a poem on their own, he encouraged them to read it aloud to themselves as part of their personal comprehension strategy. Clearly, this teacher believes that students' first encounters with a poem should be through listening.

Listening to a teacher recite a poem, joining in, and reading the poem aloud to oneself are as important in making meaning with poetry in upper grades as they are at lower levels. This is because sound is a major element in poetry. The words of a fine poem sing in the ear and echo in the mind. A poem is meant to be heard.

Because sound is at the heart of experiencing poetry, reciting a poem aloud is one of the best ways to turn students on to poetry. If the poem is a short one, listeners will be able to make meaning even as they enjoy the sound. Teachers should practice reciting aloud before sharing a poem with students; they should know the poem they are sharing so well that they can make eye contact with listeners, use gestures and facial expressions to heighten its meaning, and vary the volume and pitch of their voices. They should share a poem several times, asking students to join in on the repeating lines.

Choral speaking flows naturally out of listening to and joining in the sharing of a poem. It is an excellent way to involve students of all ages in the sounds and meanings of poetry. Having heard their teacher recite a poem, students chorus it together, not just once but several times. With each repetition, students become more familiar with the words and the meanings of a poem. They try different oral interpretations, emphasizing certain words and phrases one time and others the next time. They also begin to use their faces and bodies to express meaning. Handling a poem in this way, students get the feel for a poem and come to a deeper understanding of it.

In addition to chorusing entire short poems, other forms of choral speaking are appropriate depending on the structure and meaning of a selection. Refrain choral speaking is useful for a poem in which each stanza is followed by a repeating refrain. The teacher or a student, after practicing, renders the introductory lines of the stanza; then the total class choruses the refrain. When each line of a poem has end punctuation and requires a pause, individual students can each recite a line. In antiphonal choral speaking, the class divides into groups based on the pitch of their voices. The lower, deeper-pitched voices speak the lines that students determine should be delivered with force. The higher voices speak the lines that warrant a lighter treatment.

By the upper grades, students rather than the teacher should be able to orchestrate a piece for choral rendering. Often when deciding how to interpret a poem orally, students begin to hear the underlying sound patterns of a poem. When students try various ways to recite a poem, they often change their understanding of and feelings about it.

Another advantage to chorusing a poem repeatedly is that students quickly make the poem their own; they commit it to memory without the struggle that many teachers associate with learning poetry. In *Writing: Teachers and Children at Work* (1983), Donald Graves describes a primary classroom in which the teacher recites a poem. After just a few repetitions by the teacher and her directive, "Don't worry, just say what you remember and join in," the youngsters were reciting the poem along with the teacher. They did this without seeing the poem. As Graves explains, the teacher did not "pass out sheets for the children to read or study." She simply recited. The outcome was that the children enjoyed "the taste and beat of the words."

The same thing is possible in upper grades with short poems that have a strong beat and some repetition in words or structure. Upper-grade students enjoy making up gestures to use in interpreting a poem and often discover that using those gestures while chorusing makes it easier to remember a poem. Once students have gained ownership of a poem, the teacher can begin class by having students recite a poem or two they have learned through listening and meaningful repetition. Students often ask to chorus poems they have learned in this way and enjoy preparing videotapes of their choral renditions.

Once upper-grade students realize the pleasure to be had in playing orally with poems, they should be encouraged to use oral interpretation as a comprehension strategy when they read poetry. Instead of reading a poem silently, they read it aloud to themselves or to other students. In the process, they come to a better understanding of the poem and often a heightened enjoyment of it.

Such activity is not limited to the English or language arts classroom in the upper grades. Many poems are appropriate for other subjects, especially with the social studies. For example, a poem such as Langston Hughes' "City" belongs in a unit on the growth of cities.

In-Depth Poetry Conversations. As suggested in the first chapter, literary conversations are an integral aspect of a read aloud. By talking about ideas, students come to a better understanding of those ideas; in the process, they learn ways of reflecting on what they hear and read.

To encourage reflection, the teacher at times assumes the role of a questioner. The teacher models for students the kinds of questions they should ask themselves as they listen and read. The questions the teacher asks helps students to infer, to support inferences with evidence, and to generalize. By supporting inferences or judgments with evidence, students are making connections between general ideas and specific points. They are recognizing that an inference or judgment is weak without supporting evidence.

It is relatively easy for a teacher to guide students to think in terms of supporting evidence. Whenever a student makes an inference or renders a judgment, the teacher simply queries, "What evidence do we have for that? Let's cite specifics in support of our contention." The result is likely to be some rather sophisticated thinking.

Having asked students to cite specifics, the teacher encourages them to verbalize the steps they used in reflecting on ideas. The teacher then asks students to use those same steps in thinking about a related example. (Mr. Wexler did this when he asked students to tell him how they had gone about making meaning with "The Hippopotamus" and then asked them to do the same thing with "The Elephant.") If the teacher uses this discussion strategy on a number of occasions, students begin to provide evidence in support of ideas without being urged. They begin to demonstrate that they have learned to think in a logical way.

Oral Vocabulary Play. Students should be building their knowledge of words so that they can access them quickly as they listen and read. Unless students have considerable knowledge about words, they will have trouble reflecting in sophisticated ways on messages they are receiving. Students in Brian Wexler's seventh-grade class were acquiring four strategies for handling unfamiliar words and for expanding their vocabulary as a natural part of listening and reading:

1. using context clues to unlock word meanings.
2. making a web that highlights relationships between familiar and unfamiliar words.
3. skipping over unfamiliar words on a first attack and focusing on the overall meaning of a sentence.
4. using a dictionary after the fact to check an unfamiliar word and adding that word to a growing word web.

One strategy that encourages students to use context clues to unlock the meaning of unfamiliar words is to have them listen to sentences on familiar topics that include unfamiliar words. Knowing something about the topic, students can bring that knowledge to bear on the meaning of previously unknown words.

The teacher should use a variety of sentences in which students interpret clues in different ways. For example, in the sentence, "Hippos are aquatic, or water-dwelling, creatures," a synonym (*water-dwelling*) is juxtaposed with *aquatic*. Authors of scientific material often introduce new words by providing a synonym or an explicit definition in the sentence in which they first use the technical term. In contrast, in the sentence, "Hippos are not meat eaters; they are herbivores," the phrase *meat eaters* means the opposite of *herbivores*. Hearing this sentence, a listener must use the contrasting relationship in the sentence to understand the meaning. In the case of the sentence, "Hippos enjoy being completely submersed, only rising for breath every three or four minutes," listeners must reason from their new knowledge that hippos are aquatic to figure out that *submersed* means *under water*. At some point in an instructional sequence, teachers and students must talk about word relationships such as these.

The teacher may decide not to introduce an unfamiliar word to students before they listen to or read a selection. Mr. Wexler, for example, did not explain the word *dank* before his seventh-graders heard the Nash poem. The students listened to, enjoyed, and made meaning from the poem without knowing the meaning of this uncommonly used word.

Some students do not realize that they do not need to know all the words to understand a piece. They stop completely, sometimes trying to sound out an unfamiliar word, not realizing that they can skip over some unknown words and still get the overall sense of a paragraph or stanza from the words they do know. Good readers do not stop to sound out all the unfamiliar words or to check them in a dictionary as they read; obviously, good listeners do not do it either. At some point, upper-grade students need to make this discovery – that understanding is not dependent on knowledge of every word in a selection. This discovery leads to greater reading enjoyment; it also leads to increased reading speed.

At the same time, students should discover the pleasure in investigating unfamiliar words in a dictionary and playing with them. Mr. Wexler's seventh-graders did not find it onerous to check a dictionary for the meaning of *dank* after predicting the meaning based on context.

Some poetry buffs might be critical of Mr. Wexler and other teachers who include a formal vocabulary-building element at the beginning of or within a poetry lesson, contending that this takes the pleasure from the poetry. On the other hand, these persons rarely make the same criticism when students read stories and nonfiction selections.

It is important to teach vocabulary naturally as part of authentic reading and listening activity. Vocabulary expansion should be taught within meaningful contexts. Poetry is not fragile; a pleasurable encounter with poetry cannot be destroyed by playing with related words that build vocabulary. Even as students are enjoying the sounds and images of poetry, they can be expanding their mental lexicons.

Collaborative Learning. As noted earlier, poetry is sound; it is meant to be heard. When a team of students reads a poem together, they have the opportunity to hear the sound of it. Hearing a poem, team members get a better feeling for what the poet is trying to communicate. And when the poem is a humorous one, collaborative learning teams are even more important; humor is enjoyed much more when it is shared.

Often teachers in the upper grades rely on individual assignments rather than on group interaction and collaboration. They assign students to read a selection on their own and follow the silent reading with discussion; they assign students to write a composition without preliminary discussion of the topic. They assign homework and allocate class time to correct it. However, it is just as important to involve older students in oral language activity before they read and write as it is to involve younger students.

Collaborative learning is gaining in popularity as an instructional strategy. It is particularly appropriate when students are making meaning with poetry. We saw it in operation in Mr. Wexler's class as students read a third poem in learning teams. Functioning in teams, they completed a literature comparison chart that they had helped to structure during class discussion. Students also did not have to write alone; they could decide to write with a co-author – something very common among professional authors. Or they could work with another student to edit a previously written piece.

By writing together, students are able to hear the sounds of language that are so fundamental to good poetry (Adams and Hamm

1990). Additionally, when two students write together, both have a greater chance to succeed; words and ideas that one student generates stimulate the growth of words and ideas in the other. As a result, the co-authoring experience helps students build a more positive view of writing and of themselves as authors.

There are a great many activities in which collaborative learning is appropriate in the language arts class. Some of them include brainstorming; creating webs of interrelated words, phrases, facts, predictions, and generalizations; designing charts, maps, or graphs; compiling facts, comparative data, hypotheses, opinions, and supporting evidence; writing questions to guide reading or listening; reading a poem or story aloud to one another; discussing ideas; co-authoring a poem, short story, or informational paragraph; or revising and editing together. The attribute common to each of these activities is that, though students may be functioning with print, they also are involved fully in talking, listening, and reflecting to achieve a common goal. As an outcome, students are building oral language facility as they are learning to function as members of a team.

The Writing Workshop. During a writing workshop, all students do not work on the same assignment. Rather, students decide what they will write; writing is done for a personal purpose. During a writing workshop, students confer with other students as well as with their teacher, getting help from others by talking out problems and ideas as they prepare to write, as they work on a first draft, and as they go back to revise and edit what they have written. Near the end of a workshop, some students have the opportunity to share what they have composed with other students, who help them improve and celebrate what they have written.

Pivotal to the success of a writing workshop is the teacher-coach. It is the teacher who sets the atmosphere of cooperation during a writing workshop and who establishes the ground rules and the approach that make writing a need-fulfilling activity – even for youngsters who previously have seen writing as a source of frustration.

To achieve a positive workshop environment, teachers such as Mr. Wexler begin the year by stressing the importance of ideas in writing. They help youngsters see the joy of creating ideas by modeling the writing process. They encourage both weaker and stronger students to contribute their ideas to a class poem, as Mr. Wexler did with the cooperatively written poem about the raccoon. They leave the mechanics of writing to a later time – after students have begun to see themselves as writers of ideas and have a positive attitude toward writing.

These teachers perceive writing as a social rather than a solitary endeavor; they themselves write and share their writing and their joy in the writing process. They see talking and listening to one another as important elements in successful writing and encourage youngsters to talk together as they generate ideas, as they encounter writing problems, and as they go back to revise and edit. These teachers know that talking and listening help youngsters to go beyond the superficial to build ideas that others will want to read. In talking about ideas, young writers will begin to make connections; they will begin to compare and contrast, generalize, and formulate opinions. These teachers know that when young writers share what they have written, their writing improves. Additionally, students who listen to what their peers have composed become more critical listeners.

Assumptions About Language Arts Instruction

Mr. Wexler clearly believes in a literature-based approach to teaching language skills in which listening to literature is a significant activity. Through listening to and reflecting on poetry, upper-grade students become skillful users and pursuers of both oral and written language. Oral language activity organized around a poem provides opportunities for students to develop and refine their ability not only to listen and to speak, but to read, to write, and to use language to think.

If an observer were to ask Mr. Wexler what is the best way to teach students at the middle school level to comprehend and appreciate literature, he would probably generalize as follows:

Oral language activity before reading and writing is just as important in the upper grades as it is in the lower grades. Simply to assign students to read a selection or to write a piece without activities that tap into what they already know and that increase their vocabulary relevant to the topic is to risk making reading and writing a negative experience in students' minds.

The introduction to literature should be oral. When it is, students naturally build both listening and speaking skills. Such oral group activities as visualizing, brainstorming, webbing, and discussing are as important before students interact with poetry as they are before students interact with stories and informational selections.

The best introduction to a poem is listening to it. When listening to a poem, students can hear the sounds that make the poem a joy to experience; they also may find it easier to make meaning with it. Upper-grade students who read a poem independently should be encouraged to read the poem aloud to themselves or to chorus the poem with members of a learning team. Poems are meant to be heard.

Upper-grade students enjoy joining in as they listen to a poem. In doing so, they come to a heightened appreciation of the sounds of the poem. They also enjoy repeating a poem on numerous occasions, joining in as the teacher recites it. If the poem is a short one, students will quickly and painlessly make the poem their own.

Emphasis in listening should be on helping students to make the poem have personalized meanings. Emphasis also should be on helping students to support their inferences and judgments with details. Compiling literary comparison charts is one way to make meaning after listening.

As students listen to poems, they should be expanding their mental lexicons by learning to decipher unfamiliar words through context clues, word-structure clues, and dictionary searches. They need reassurance that they do not have to know each and every word to enjoy listening to or reading a poem.

It is important to organize learning activities in "wholes." One way to do this is through focus units containing several selections that share a common element. This makes it easier for students to reflect on content in a variety of ways – by comparing and contrasting, by generalizing, by generating opinions. Teachers should model how to make these kinds of meanings by involving students orally in interrelated unit activities with poems as well as with stories and nonfiction selections.

Collaborative learning activities provide meaningful contexts for refining listening and speaking skills. When students function as members of a learning team, they must interact orally to achieve group objectives.

The teaching of listening in the upper grades should not be isolated from the teaching of writing. Writing at this level should be viewed as a social process. The teacher must encourage students to write and then share what they have drafted. The outcome of such purposeful communication is heightened ability to listen to and reflect on ideas, as well as a more positive attitude toward writing.

Just as the teaching of listening in the upper grades should be integrated with the teaching of writing, so should it be integrated with the teaching of reading. In both, the emphasis is on thinking, on making meaning. A natural, integrated approach is the best way to teach reflective listening. Students learn to listen through interacting with literature, listening to a piece being read or recited aloud, thinking and talking together about that piece, writing collaboratively after listening and talking, and reading together in learning teams to apply their understanding and skill. In learning to listen and reflect, students are learning to read and reflect.

References

Adams, Dennis, and Hamm, Mary. *Cooperative Learning: Critical Thinking and Collaboration Across the Curriculum*. Springfield, Ill.: Charles C. Thomas, 1990.

Graves, Donald. *Writing: Teachers and Children at Work*. Portsmouth, N.H.: Heinemann Educational Books, 1983.

Moss, Joy. *Focus Units in Literature: A Handbook for Elementary Teachers*. Urbana, Ill.: National Council of Teachers of English, 1984.

4

A READ ALOUD WITH NONFICTION:

REFLECTIVE LISTENING IN FOURTH GRADE

In this chapter, you will meet Steve Lugo and his class of fourth-graders. You will observe the students listening to, talking about, and writing in response to two nonfiction trade books. As you read about these young people and their teacher, again consider the objectives the teacher has in mind, the strategies he uses to achieve his objectives, and the assumptions he holds about teaching listening and reading to young people.

Tricks with Language and Sight

Mr. Lugo began his lesson: "Today, boys and girls, I am going to read from a book called *Tomfoolery: Trickery and Foolery with Words*. It is by a highly respected author of informational books, Alvin Schwartz. Look at the cover. Look at the title as I have written it on the board. Let's do what we always do before listening to a selection – use the cover and the title to get clues as to what the selection is about. What do you think the word *tomfoolery* means?"

Using the context clue Schwartz built into the title, the students proposed that tomfoolery has to do with word tricks, with ways of fooling around with words. Without prompting, one student checked the dictionary and read the definition given there, "Foolish or silly behavior, a silly act, matter, or thing." The class, however, decided that the topic of the book is narrower than that implied by the dictionary definition. They could tell from the clue Schwartz supplied in the second half of the title. One student went to the board to darken the colon between the two parts of the title. The class talked about the meaning of this mark of punctuation – that it is a mark that sets up an equation in the sentence. In this case, tomfoolery is equivalent to trickery and foolery with words. One student mapped the relationship on the board:

tomfoolery = trickery and foolery with words

The students concluded that this is a book about playing jokes with words.

Then Mr. Lugo asked, "Can anyone give an example of trickery and foolery with words?" Because no one could think of an example, the teacher said, "Well, listen to this. It may prompt your memory." Then he shared the following folk rhyme:

As I was going to St. Ives,
I met a man with seven wives.
Each wife had seven sacks;
Each sack had seven cats;
Each cat had seven kits:
Kits, cats, sacks, and wives,
How many were going to St. Ives?

As soon as he had finished, students called out, "Read it again, Mr. Lugo"; and so he did, admonishing the fourth-graders to think carefully. Students listened, thought, and wrote their answers on slips of paper. Then they argued. Some argued that there were 28 going to St. Ives – seven wives, seven sacks, seven cats, and seven kits. Some argued that there were 21 – you couldn't count the sacks because they were not people or animals. Some argued that the man had to be included in the count. Some argued that the answer was one, because no man, kits, cats, sacks, or wives were going; only the speaker was going. Some argued that the answer was none since the question (Kits, cats, sacks, and wives/How many were going to St. Ives?) asked only about the kits, cats, sacks, and wives.

The teacher asked, "Why may this piece of folklore be called tomfoolery?" Students proposed that it is a trick with words; it probably was written to trick the listener.

One student then said, "I know another example." This youngster shared a favorite knock-knock joke. Other students quickly got the point; and since they all knew some knock-knocks, they also shared them. One student then recited, "How much wood would a wood-chuck chuck?" and asked if that is an example of tomfoolery. The others decided that it was.

Surveying and Predicting

With that as an introduction, the teacher said, "OK. Let's begin. I am going to read aloud the first paragraph from the jacket flap. As I read, listen to see if our prediction about the content of the book is on target." The teacher then read aloud:

> Here is a book full of tricks to amuse, confuse, and bamboozle your family and friends. These are not tricks which involve hiding someone's lunch or nailing his sneakers to the floor, these are word tricks which depend on verbal hocus-pocus.

Students decided that they were partly right about the focus of the book: This book is about tricks with words; however, it does not just explain tomfoolery with words but contains lots of examples.

Mr. Lugo then read aloud the next paragraph from the jacket flap and asked students to listen for kinds of word tricks. The paragraph describes tricks that make people feel silly when they give the right answer, riddles with ridiculous answers, tall talk, endless tales, and tales with tricky endings. As students recalled these five kinds of tricks, a scribe recorded them on the chalkboard.

Then the teacher asked, "If you were going to give examples of these kinds of word tricks, what would be a good way of organizing them? Would you just lump them all together?" The students rapidly agreed that they would probably have a section for each kind of trick. Mr. Lugo responded, "Let's see how Schwartz did it."

With that, the teacher showed the table of contents. Students predicted that the first chapter ("If Frozen Water Is Iced Water, What Is Frozen Ink?") contains tricks that make people feel silly when they give the right answer. They predicted that the second chapter ("What Is Black and Red All Over?") contains riddles with crazy answers. They made similar predictions for the other three chapters.

The teacher said, "Sometimes before reading an informational book like this one, it pays to do a quick survey to see if you are on the right track. Let's just turn to the introduction to each chapter and see if our predictions are accurate." Aloud, Mr. Lugo read the very short introduction to each chapter. The students had accurately predicted the content of each.

Then the teacher said, "Now let me read the short introductory chapter to you. As you listen, keep in mind important main idea-making questions: What is this author trying to tell us? What is the big idea the author wants to get across to the readers? Introductory sections often supply us with this kind of information." Aloud, Mr. Lugo read the section.

Having listened, the students noted that the introduction to the book contains some of the same information about kinds of word tricks found on the jacket flaps. It also contains some details about how folklore is passed from person to person. They decided that the main idea of the book is that there are many kinds of word tricks. The teacher recorded the students' anticipated main idea in a horizontal block he had drawn on the board.

Then he turned to the first chapter and asked, "What did we decide was the point of this chapter?" Students remembered that the chapter deals with word foolery in which there is a trap that makes someone look silly. Mr. Lugo recorded that statement in a vertical block attached to the anticipated main idea. Students then recalled the main point of the other four chapters. A scribe recorded a main idea statement for each chapter on the board in a vertical box attached to the anticipated main idea. (See Figure 5.)

Mr. Lugo summed up what the class had been doing. He said, "You know, it often pays to survey a book in the way we have done before reading. The survey gives you a framework for thinking about what is in the book. It helps you plan and organize your reading."

Listening with a Purpose

"Now," Mr. Lugo asked, "about what kind of word trick do you want me to read first? With this kind of book, you do not have to read from the beginning. You can skip around in it." Students wanted to start with the riddles, and so Mr. Lugo began by sharing some of them. Students attempted answers before Mr. Lugo read them from the book. In the same way, Mr. Lugo read samples of the other kinds of word plays. Wherever possible, he encouraged students to join in on the answers or on repeating lines.

The students enjoyed hearing examples of tomfoolery. When they had listened to several examples of each kind, Mr. Lugo said, "Do you remember what we proposed as the main point the author was trying to communicate? Do you think that there is more to it than that?"

Figure 5. A graphic organizer for thinking about main ideas.

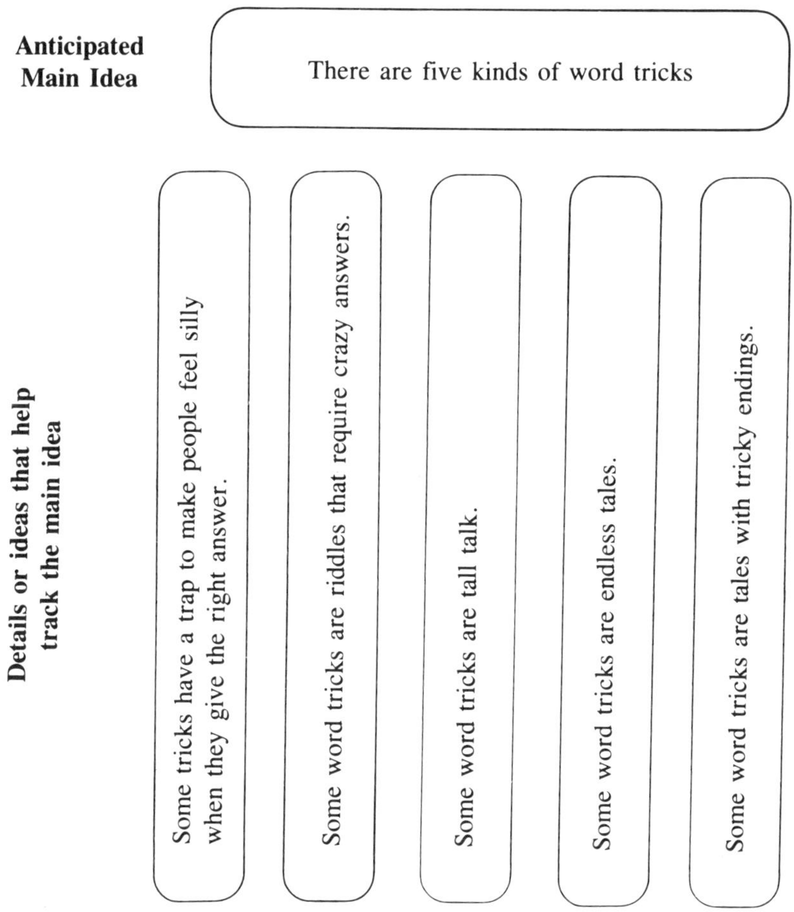

The students talked about the tricks they had heard. Together they decided that, while the author wanted them to know that there were five kinds of word trickery, he also wanted them to know that it is fun to fool with words. Students recorded this as the main idea in the graphic organizer they had been developing.

Summarizing After Listening

Mr. Lugo then shifted gears; he said, "Let's use our graphic organizer to draft a paragraph summarizing the main points of

Schwartz's book. Give me the main idea of the book. Then give me the supporting details. You can read them right off our main-idea organizer." As the students dictated sentences, the teacher recorded them on the board. Then the students consolidated and revised until they had a final paragraph:

> There are five major kinds of word trickery. One kind involves questions that make people feel silly when they give the right answers. A second kind is the riddle. There are also word plays called tall talk, endless tales, and tales with tricky endings. It is fun to listen to word tricks.

The teacher asked the students how their summary paragraph resembled their graphic organizer. Students saw that the organizer and the paragraph had a similar structure and that this structure paralleled Alvin Schwartz's in *Tomfoolery*.

Mr. Lugo told his students that there are many more examples of word tricks in Schwartz's book. He placed the book in the reading center and suggested that students read other sections of it on their own and select an example or two to share with the class.

Considering Visual Trickery

On the next afternoon, Mr. Lugo began a related lesson by displaying a chart with the visual shown in Figure 6.

Figure 6. The optical illusion used by Mr. Lugo to introduce his unit on the book, *The Optical Illusion Book*, by Seymour Simon.

He told his fourth-graders to stare at the visual. Students quickly got the point; they explained that, as they stared, the "opening" in the circles shifted from right to left and back again. Mr. Lugo asked, "Does anyone know what we call this kind of trick?" Some students were able to name the trick as an optical illusion. The teacher asked, "What is the meaning of the word *optical*? What is the meaning of the word *illusion*?" The students suggested definitions. One boy checked a dictionary to see if they were right, and cooperatively the class mapped an equation defining the term optical illusion.

optical illusion = something you see that is not exactly what is there

Then the students proposed other examples of optical illusions they already knew. One described a mirage, and at the teacher's prompting wrote the word *mirage* on the chalkboard.

With that as a brief introduction, Mr. Lugo announced, "Today I am going to share parts of another book. In some ways the material in it is similar to that in *Tomfoolery: Trickery and Foolery with Words*. In other ways the material is different. The book is called *The Optical Illusion Book*. It is by Seymour Simon, who, like Alvin Schwartz, has written many informational books. Before I actually read the book, what should I do?"

Students recalled what they had done with the Schwartz book and suggested looking at the jacket flap and the introduction to see if those parts could give them some understanding of the author's main idea. The teacher read aloud information from the jacket flaps. Based on it, the students proposed what they had begun to call their anticipated main idea – that there are many ways the eye can be tricked into seeing things that are not really there. They also suggested the author's purpose – to explain some of these tricks.

After that, Mr. Lugo read the introduction – "Seeing is Believing." As he read it aloud, he asked the students to follow along on a copy that he displayed with the overhead projector from a transparency he had made from the text. He explained, "As I read, I am going to tell you the thoughts that go through my head. When I listen or read, I keep my mind active; and I want to show you the ways I do this."

Simultaneously reading and thinking aloud, the teacher did such things as answering the questions raised in the text, telling himself about the figures, telling himself a definition, commenting on the ideas, paraphrasing the text, and asking questions. He also said aloud to himself, "This book is going to be like Alvin Schwartz's because both are about tricks. This book is different, however, because it deals with visual tricks, not word tricks."

When the teacher had finished reading aloud and demonstrating how he uses mind talk to make meaning while reading, he asked the students to recall the kinds of things he had done so that he could write them on the board as a chart. To help the students, Mr. Lugo repeated some of his thoughts. Together they devised the chart in Figure 7.

At the end of the introduction to the book, Seymour Simon suggests that readers try to reproduce the drawing of one optical illusion. Mr. Lugo displayed a particularly tricky optical illusion with

Figure 7. A chart to guide thinking while listening.

Kind of thinking	How I used this kind of thinking
Answering questions in the text	When the author asked, "Do you believe everything you see?" I said, "No."
Telling oneself about a figure	I talked to myself to interpret the length of the lines in the first figure.
Repeating a definition	I told myself the meaning of optical illusion.
Making comments about the ideas	When I read that there are some optical illusions in nature, I said to myself, "A mirage is one."
Asking questions	I asked at one point, "Which figure does he mean?"
Stating the ideas in one's own words	I paraphrased the two kinds of optical illusions after reading about them.
Comparing and contrasting	I compared the book by Simon to the one by Schwartz.

an overhead projector and gave his students time to draw. Most students had some difficulty drawing and visualizing. As a result, they decided that some optical illusions are very sophisticated.

Mr. Lugo turned the page to the first chapter, "How You See." He told his class, "Based on this picture of the eye and the title, what is this chapter about?" Students agreed that the chapter tells how the eye functions. The teacher said, "I want to learn about optical illusions. I do not think that I want to think now about the way the eye works. Therefore, I am going to skip the first chapter and go to the second, 'Why You See Optical Illusions.' Don't think you have to read every part of a book like this. It is perfectly OK to skip parts."

The teacher then projected the first page of the next chapter so that the students could follow along as he read aloud. He read paragraph by paragraph, stopping periodically for students to record their thoughts on a chart. Finishing the short chapter, Mr. Lugo had the students tell what they thought as they listened to the chapter. He also had the students sum up the main idea of the chapter. He had them explain in their own words why people see optical illusions. Doing this, the teacher explained how important it is in listening and reading to stop from time to time to tell ourselves the important ideas.

On the next afternoon, Mr. Lugo again picked up *The Optical Illusion Book*. He read the titles of the remaining chapters aloud to the class and displayed some of the illustrations. He asked the students to predict from the titles and some of the figures what each chapter is about. Then he announced, "I will not have time to read all the chapters aloud to you. Based on your predictions, let us decide what chapter to hear today." Because the students remembered the circular optical illusion that their teacher had displayed earlier (Figure 6), most of the students wanted to hear the chapter called "Changeable Figures" that contains that illustration.

Before reading the chapter, Mr. Lugo asked his fourth-graders what they wanted to learn from that chapter. Students responded by raising two questions they hoped to answer: What exactly is a changeable figure? How does a changeable figure work?

And so Mr. Lugo propped himself against his desk, told the students to keep their two questions in mind, and began to read aloud. This time the students did not follow along with the text. They had to find the answers to their questions by reflecting while listening.

Having listened, students paused for a moment to try to write an answer to their first question (What is a changeable figure?) in their learning logs. Mr. Lugo suggested that they start by writing a sentence with a definition and then continue by composing a sentence or two that describe an example. He suggested that in introducing the example they begin their sentence with the phrase, *for example*. On the board he mapped the relationship among the ideas to be drafted.

As the students wrote, Mr. Lugo circulated, giving help to students who had trouble beginning. Volunteers then read their paragraphs. Since the chapter in *The Optical Illusion Book* on changeable figures presents a number of examples, students' paragraphs were different. Listeners discussed the different ways in which the students defined *changeable figure* and the examples they had chosen to clarify their definitions. After several of the young authors had shared their paragraphs, students reviewed the structure of the paragraphs they had written: definition followed by sentences describing an example.

The teacher asked students if they remembered the second question they had raised before listening. Students remembered the "why" question and proposed answers based on the text. Mr. Lugo reminded the students that when an answer to a question is rather complicated, as in this case, it pays to tell oneself the answer by making mind talk.

To make students aware of the listening and reading comprehension strategies that they had been using (in other words, to build metacognitive awareness), the teacher next had the students think about what they had just done. He helped them to recall that they had started by surveying the book to decide what part to read. They had continued by using the chapter title and the illustrations to raise questions to answer through listening. Having listened, they first had written a summary paragraph that answered one question and then had told themselves the answer to the second. Mr. Lugo suggested that this was a workable approach for reading nonfiction.

Working Cooperatively

The next afternoon, Mr. Lugo divided his class into four six-person learning teams. He did this because he had only four copies of the Simon book, and he wanted each team to work cooperatively to apply the comprehension strategy that they had learned the previous day. Members of a team selected one chapter, surveyed that chapter, and wrote at least two questions in their learning logs to answer through reading. Then they took turns reading their assigned chapter aloud to their team. In each case, two students were to view the text and were to read aloud in unison. As the students read, the other team members were to listen to find answers. They could stop at any time in the reading to discuss the questions and suggest answers. After reading their chapter, the students re-grouped into co-authoring teams and wrote a paragraph using the definition-example structure. The teacher suggested that students on a team might want to make a drawing to clarify their paragraphs.

The following day, Mr. Lugo scheduled a sharing time. Co-authoring teams orally shared their paragraphs. After each team had read its paragraph, listeners paraphrased the definitions included in it and identified the example or examples the co-authors had used. Mr. Lugo reminded students that when reading nonfiction, it often pays to do just what they had been doing – take time to write a paragraph summarizing important ideas.

The Teacher's Objectives and Strategies

What were Mr. Lugo's objectives in planning and teaching this focus unit with the books *Tomfoolery* and *The Optical Illusion Book*? What did he hope the students would learn?

Mr. Lugo's primary objective was that the fourth-graders enjoy listening to, reading, and thinking about informational content. He hoped that the students would learn to love nonfiction and ask him to share more of these kinds of books that they could read on their own.

In addition, Mr. Lugo hoped his students would learn to handle nonfiction when they heard and read it. More specifically, he wanted them to learn to use information from the cover, the jacket flaps, and the introduction as a framework for activating their related knowledge before listening or reading, for predicting before listening or reading, and for making decisions about what to listen to or read in a book. He wanted them to learn to raise questions that would guide their listening and reading, to answer those questions, and to compose a summary paragraph that addressed one or more of the questions they had raised. In short, Mr. Lugo was helping his students to acquire basic comprehension strategies.

Mr. Lugo hoped his students would understand that nonfiction has a structure, or an organization, and would be able to use their understanding of structure to comprehend more fully. He wanted them to realize that many pieces of nonfiction have an introduction that gives an overview, that nonfiction books are organized into chapters in a logical way, and that paragraphs have a structure. In this case, the teacher hoped that students would come away with an understanding of one paragraph design – definition followed by example – and be able to compose as well as comprehend paragraphs with that structure.

Mr. Lugo also stressed the importance of making mind talk while listening and reading. He hoped his students would be able to use mind talk to answer questions proposed by an author in a text, to explain any visuals in the text, to paraphrase important definitions and ideas, to raise questions, to make comparisons, and to summarize.

Last, but not least, Mr. Lugo wanted his students to refine their ability to listen and speak during informal interaction. He wanted them to learn to listen to one another as they worked together in learning teams; he wanted them to learn to listen respectfully to reports given by their classmates and to be able to identify key information contained in the reports.

How did Steve Lugo achieve his objectives? He used a variety of strategies, including a read aloud, a nonfiction-based conversation, a think aloud, prediction while listening, mapping, and response writing, specifically summarizing and paraphrasing. Let us consider each of these, focusing especially on the way the strategies provide opportunity for students to reflect as they listen.

A Nonfiction Read Aloud. James Squire (1984) writes: "The skills required to read science must be acquired through reading science. The skills required in writing science can be learned only by writing science. Basic reading and writing instruction can provide children with rudimentary vocabulary and certain basic skills of literacy, but application to higher levels of processing requires specialized uses." As Squire further explains, children need to be taught to apply their comprehension skills "to a variety of subject matters." This is important because "skills have unique and particular relevance to every discipline."

Although Squire is addressing reading and writing instruction, the same case can be made for listening. Students need opportunity to listen to all manner of content material with attention to the ways in which different kinds of nonfiction are organized and developed. This attention pays dividends in terms of growth in reading as well as in listening comprehension.

What are good kinds of nonfictional materials for sharing orally with students at the elementary and junior high school levels? Mr. Lugo's focus unit provides an answer. For reading aloud nonfiction with young students, the teacher should select content that is not overly technical and that has a natural appeal to students of that age. With older students, the teacher also can explore controversial questions in which students have a difference of opinion (Carter and Abrahamson 1991).

Good sources of nonfiction for read alouds are weekly newspapers published for students, editorials from local newspapers, and newspaper stories. Teachers have successfully shared articles about President Bush's dislike for broccoli, the declining population of foxes, the training of elephants, and censorship of children's books.

Teachers also can organize a read aloud based on a segment from a trade book or from a reference such as an encyclopedia, an atlas, or an almanac. The appropriate time to use this material is within a unit in the natural sciences, in the social sciences, or in health. Students listen to find answers to questions they have raised as part of their study. Based on what they already know and on what they want to know, students decide what parts of the selections the teacher should read aloud and what parts to skip. In so doing, they learn the skill of selective reading, skipping around in a text to get information and skipping over text judged to be unrelated to one's reading purpose.

Teachers and students can use textbooks in a similar way. Rather than always reading chapters in their science or social studies texts, at times students listen with a well-conceived purpose as their teacher reads a chapter or parts of one. This approach adds variety to content-area instruction; it also gives the teacher an opportunity to teach comprehension strategies by modeling for students how to make meaning with nonfiction.

Questioning/Answering Patterns. Questioning is a major weapon in a teacher's instructional arsenal. It is a particularly effective strategy to encourage reflective thinking as part of a nonfiction-based read aloud and conversation. This is true at every level of instruction.

Here are some ways to vary questioning so that students learn not only to get information from nonfiction but also to raise questions to guide their own listening and reading of informational content:

1. Surveying for Questions Before Listening. Before reading a piece of nonfiction aloud to a group of students, the teacher helps them to survey the piece by drawing their attention to the title, the subheads, the introductory segments, and the illustrations. Having surveyed these key structural elements, students propose questions, which

a scribe records on the chalkboard while the students write them in their learning logs. As they listen, students jot down answers to the questions. At the end of the selection, students read their answers aloud and talk about their findings.

When first using this strategy, the teacher may find it necessary to model the process of writing answers to questions after listening. The teacher reads a segment that answers a question raised during the preliminary survey and then stops. Students and the teacher cooperate in devising an answer to the question, and a scribe records the answer on the chalkboard while the students record it in their learning logs. The next time the teacher reads a segment that provides an answer and then stops at the end to give students time to write down their response. Students and teacher discuss possible responses before moving on.

2. Raising Questions for the Teacher. Another approach is for the teacher to read aloud a segment of text, stopping periodically for students to write down questions that were answered in that segment. After reading, the teacher closes the book and sits back to be questioned by the students. The students simply read the questions they have recorded in their learning logs, and the teacher tries to answer them. When the teacher cannot answer, the questioner gives the answer; and the teacher orally re-reads the sentences that verify the answer.

3. Answering Teacher-Posed Questions. Often when students first try their hand at raising questions, they tend to be simple factual questions; rarely do they ask questions of the teacher that require in-depth thinking. At this point, the teacher raises some more thoughtful questions for students to answer and asks them to compare these kinds of question with those the children have raised. The teacher encourages: "Try modeling the questions you ask after mine. Try to stump me by asking questions that do not have answers found directly in the text."

4. Raising Questions for Other Students. Students also may raise questions for their peers. This kind of interaction can be organized as a game, with students grouped into teams that take turns asking questions based on a segment of text they have heard. A correct answer – and the teacher serves as the judge of correctness – wins a point for the answering team. Organized in this way, the activity encourages students to devise difficult questions that require in-depth thinking.

Another activity is to divide students into data collectors and interrogators. As students listen to a segment of text, data collectors record as many important points as they can. At the same time, interrogators devise questions about that segment of text. After the teacher has read the segment, interrogators ask their questions in an attempt to stump the data collectors. For the next segment of text, data collectors and interrogators change roles. To make this approach work, the teacher will have to model for students not only how to raise questions that go beyond the text but also how to take notes while listening.

An advantage of these activities is that the instruction mirrors for students an effective comprehension strategy. Raising and answering questions as one listens or reads is a good way to monitor one's own comprehension.

A Think Aloud. A second major weapon in a teacher's instructional arsenal that is particularly useful in encouraging reflection is the "think aloud." As pointed out in Chapter 1, think alouds are a way to demonstrate how a listener or reader makes meaning with text. In using the strategy, the teacher reads a segment of text aloud to a group of children and interjects the thoughts that come to mind in reference to that text (see Chapter 1, pages 22-23).

In his lesson on optical illusions, Mr. Lugo made use of the think aloud strategy. Because students did not have their own copies of the book to which to refer as they listened, Mr. Lugo projected the page on the screen. He did this to distinguish what words were actual text and what words were his thoughts in response.

Mr. Lugo also relied on an approach suggested by Beth Davey. After his think aloud, the teacher had his students review the kinds of thoughts he had made; and together they devised a chart that listed kinds of thoughts to make while listening or reading. In this fourth-grade class, the chart listed: 1) answering questions in the text, 2) telling about a figure, 3) repeating a definition, 4) stating the ideas in one's own words, 5) commenting on the ideas, 6) asking questions, and 7) comparing and contrasting. Other items that can appear on charts include: 1) forming pictures in the mind (visualizing), 2) linking what is being heard or read to what is already known, 3) predicting, 4) evaluating and judging, and 5) clarifying and correcting errors in comprehension made earlier (Davey 1983).

Once students have heard their teacher share a piece in a think aloud, they can try the technique themselves. One way is for students to work in two-person teams. One student reads a segment to the listener and interjects think aloud mind talk. Using a chart like the one described above, the other student listens and identifies the kinds of thoughts the reader is making. The reader and listener then shift roles with another short selection. As a follow-up, students can read a text to themselves and carry on their own think aloud. Later they use the chart to identify the kinds of thoughts they made.

Prediction. One kind of thinking that is particularly important in making meaning with nonfiction, and which a teacher should model at some point, is predicting or anticipating. Many educators advocate that students be taught to make predictions before and while reading. The predictions provide a framework for interpreting incoming data.

Russell Stauffer (1969) emphasizes the importance of predictions in comprehending a text. He advocates that listeners and readers of nonfiction be taught to speculate on the topic and content of a selection. When reading fiction, students should be taught to anticipate what a story is about, what will happen in it, and how the story ends. An ideal place to teach prediction is during a read aloud.

Patricia and James Cunningham (1987) propose that students construct a grid, called a "feature matrix," as a means of speculating before interacting with text. Before reading, students speculate on the characteristics of things they will encounter in a selection. Next to each characteristic, readers record their prediction. The result is a table of predictions. As students read, they refer to their table and correct their predictions as they go along. These grids are useful for predicting before listening as well as before reading, and they also are useful for generalizing after listening and reading.

Hennings (1991) proposes that before reading a selection, students should be encouraged to use a variety of clues to predict, or target, the major point the author is trying to make. Students can find clues to the main idea in the title, the subheads, the illustrations, the introductory paragraphs, and the concluding paragraphs. Having targeted a point before reading or listening, students then track the point. Tracking a point means keeping the anticipated main idea in mind, using that idea to judge the significance of details, and modifying the anticipated idea as new information comes to light. As students think about the point, they relate it to what they already know and to the personal significance it has for them. Emphasis in this strategy, called "essential reading," is on making the main idea clear.

Figure 8. A feature matrix used for listening to a geography book.

Directions: Before listening to or reading about the countries listed below, predict their characteristics. Put a + in the box if you predict that a country has that characteristic. Put a – in the box if you predict it does not. If you have no idea, leave the box empty. Listen or read to test your predictions. Add characteristics to the matrix as you proceed. Generalize after you listen or read.

Characteristics identified before listening/reading	**Japan**	**Iran**	**Saudi Arabia**	**Russia**	**Great Britain**
1. is a major oil producer					
2. is a major oil consumer					
3. is a major industrial nation					
4. has a population greater than 10 million					
5. is located in the northern hemisphere					
6. is located in the western hemisphere					
7. is a democracy					
Characteristics identified while listening/reading					
1.					
2.					

Generalizations formed after listening/reading:

1. Japan is a country that
2. Iran is a country that
3. Saudi Arabia is a country that
4. Russia is a country that
5. Great Britain is a country that

The teaching/learning vignette at the beginning of this chapter provides an example of how a teacher can model essential reading during a read aloud. Before students listened to parts of Alvin Schwartz's book on word foolery, Mr. Lugo had them survey the chapters and predict the main point of the book and of the individual chapters. He had them plot their predictions on paper; then he shared parts of the book with the class, asking the students to keep their anticipated main ideas in mind. Finally, having talked about the selection with them, he had the students check their predictions and come up with a summary sentence about what the author was driving at. His emphasis was on targeting the main idea before reading, tracking it while reading, and thinking about it after reading.

Mapping. To comprehend nonfiction, listeners and readers must be able not only to use prediction to guide thinking but also to perceive the logical relationship among ideas. For example, a writer very often starts with a sentence stating a general point or a definition. Then the writer supports the general point or definition with an example that clarifies the overarching point of that segment of text. Encountering this type of content, listeners and readers may visualize the relationship among the ideas and recognize what the author is doing.

A strategy for clarifying relationships among ideas is the logic map, like the one in Figure 5 on page 69. By having students map logical relationships in this way, the teacher is preparing them to take notes on ideas they receive orally. Since much instruction in high school and college is through lectures, upper-grade teachers must help students develop note-taking skills.

A more generalized form of mapping is similar to the common outline, where the student writes the main idea at the top and lists supporting details underneath. Students begin by drawing blocks around the main idea and each supporting detail. This is best used with deductively organized material, where the author starts with a main point and then lists examples. A variation can be used to clarify the structure of inductively organized content in which an author starts by presenting a series of details. Students can compare paragraphs organized deductively to those organized inductively, talk about relationships, and draw a diagram that makes those relationships explicit. In doing this, students begin to see that just as stories and poems have a design or structure, so does informational writing. They begin to see that they can use this structure to help them make meaning as they listen and read.

In some cases, the author does not explicitly state a main idea but simply lists a series of related details. Listeners or readers must make the leap from details to generalization. The teacher can help students to make that leap by stopping and asking, "What do these facts mean? What do they tell us? What is this author getting at by presenting all these details?" Students can add their inferred main idea to their logic map.

After students have mastered making logic maps, they can take the next step and simply record main ideas with supporting details without drawing blocks around them. Teachers may take this opportunity to clarify the steps of formal outlining using Roman and Arabic numerals and lower- and upper-case letters by superimposing numerals and letters on the logic maps the students have been creating. However, teachers must make students aware that there are many ways to take notes on material being heard or read. A formal outline is only one way, which may or may not serve a student's purpose in a particular instance.

Logic maps focus on relationships between main and subordinate ideas. Of course, there are other kinds of relationships among ideas. Again, visualizing through mapping can help students to see how ideas fit together. Here are some examples of other kinds of relationships with ways to help students visualize the logic inherent in them.

1. Definitions. Write these as an equation with an equal sign between a term and its definition.
2. Cause-and-effect relationships. Use arrows to connect causes, or reasons, to their effects, or outcomes.
3. Chronological sequences. Use time lines to show the sequence.
4. Hierarchies and categories. Use concentric circles to clarify hierarchical relationships and web-like visuals to highlight categories.
5. Comparisons and contrasts. Use a chart-like arrangement with parallel columns to indicate differences. Do the same for similarities.
6. Concluding, generalizing, or judging. Use a graphic organizer that shows the flow of specific pieces of data into the conclusion or generalization. Use similar graphics to highlight the relationship between supporting evidence and an opinion.

Response Writing – Summarizing and Paraphrasing. Research indicates that one of the best ways to learn material heard or read is to write a summary of it or paraphrase it (Day 1980; Taylor 1982; Cunningham 1982). As Devine (1986) explains, "The process of writing about what they have read [or heard] is one of the most effective means students have of discovering their texts-in-their-heads." In writing a summary, a person concisely restates the main idea of a communication and key supporting evidence. In paraphrasing a text, students tell in their own words what a writer is driving at.

Teacher-guided group writing following a read aloud is an instructional approach for teaching students how to write a summary or to paraphrase a message. To teach summary writing, the teacher shares a piece of nonfiction and then asks, "What is the main point this author is trying to communicate?" Several students suggest what they believe is the main idea. Drawing on the ideas suggested, students and the teacher compose one sentence that becomes the topic sentence in a summary paragraph drafted by the class. The teacher follows with this question, "What are the important pieces of supporting evidence that the author offers?" Again, students suggest possibilities, which may be recorded on the chalkboard. Selecting from the brainstormed list of possible points, students and the teacher compose sentences to add to their written summary.

A slightly different approach to summary writing is the one demonstrated in the lesson that opens this chapter. In this case, the teacher and students first made a graphic organizer that highlighted major and subordinate ideas. This organizer, or map, became the students' outline for composing their summary paragraph.

Because a summary should be concise, students and their teacher often must go back to edit and revise what they have composed together. In this context, the teacher can encourage students to look for:

- entire sentences that are redundant and that can be deleted;
- individual words that can be deleted;
- sentences that can be combined.

Once a teacher has modeled summary writing after listening, students can work in learning teams to write summaries based on content they have heard. In this case, a teacher may find it useful to ask students to write the final drafts of their summaries on chart paper or on acetate for display with an overhead projector. If several learning teams share their products, the students can compare the summaries. They may be able to identify different ways in which they can make their summaries more concise.

Also, students can work independently after reading to write their own summaries. This gives students the opportunity to apply a skill – summary writing – in a different way.

A similar instructional sequence can be used to teach paraphrasing:

- Students listen as the teacher shares an article.
- Students and the teacher work together to paraphrase the article. They record their version as a chart.
- The class cooperatively revises and edits the paragraph, particularly asking, "Have we told in our own words what the author is getting at?"
- Students listen as the teacher shares a related article.
- Students work in learning teams to paraphrase the second article.
- Students read a similar kind of article.
- Students paraphrase the article, first by telling a peer what they think the author is getting at and then by individually writing what they think on paper.

Assumptions About Learning to Listen, Reflect, and Read

Mr. Lugo's lesson sequence provides clues as to what this teacher holds important in teaching students to listen, to reflect, and to read. Rather clearly, this teacher – like Ms. O'Dell and Mr. Wexler – believes in teaching language skills through meaningful interaction with an authentic text. He believes that as students listen to and reflect on nonfiction, they develop as skillful users of both oral and written language. In short, students become better listeners, better readers, better comprehenders of ideas by listening to and talking about nonfiction.

If an observer were to ask Mr. Lugo what is the best way to teach students to comprehend and appreciate expository writing, he would probably generalize as follows:

There is no one best way to teach students to comprehend and appreciate expository writing. Students should be given opportunities to interact with texts in a variety of ways.

Teachers should read nonfiction aloud just as they read aloud stories and poems. A read aloud followed by discussion provides many contexts for thinking about nonfiction.

Teachers should model how they do mind talk in response to a text heard or read. One way to do this is for teachers to read aloud and talk out the thoughts that come to mind. In the same way, teachers should encourage students to engage in mind talk in response to a selection.

Raising questions prior to listening to or reading expository text and then listening or reading to construct answers increases comprehension. Teachers should not ask all the questions. They should demonstrate for students the variety of questions readers and listeners can raise in response to a text; they should organize instruction so that students begin to raise their own questions about a text.

Prediction is tremendously important in reading expository text. Students should be taught how to survey a text to predict what it is about, how it is organized, and what the main idea is. They should use their pre-reading speculations to guide their reading. Again, teachers should model ways of predicting and encourage students to predict as they read and as they listen.

One way to reflect on expository texts is to map the relationships among ideas. Teachers should read aloud content that is organized deductively (a general statement followed by supporting details) and organized inductively (supporting details followed by a general statement), requiring readers to infer the main idea. They should share definitions, statements of cause and effect, chronological sequences, statements that indicate hierarchical and categorical relations, statements of comparison and contrast, and judgments. Working with a variety of texts, teachers should demonstrate step-by-step how to clarify these relationships through mapping.

Writing about ideas helps comprehension. Teachers should model how to paraphrase and how to write a summary after listening or reading. An effective way to handle this is teacher-guided group writing and editing. Having participated in a teacher-guided writing activity, students should apply what they have learned by writing in learning teams and on their own after listening to or reading a piece of nonfiction.

Through listening to and talking about text, students acquire strategies for comprehending text. This means that students not only become better listeners but also become better readers, since reflection is what both listening and reading are all about. Although there are some elements of listening and reading that are distinctive to each, there is a large area of overlap relating to basic aspects of thinking.

References

Carter, Betty, and Abrahamson, Richard. "Nonfiction in a Read-Aloud Program." *Journal of Reading* 34 (May 1991): 638-42.

Cunningham, J.W. "Generating Interactions Between Schemata and Text." In *New Inquiries in Reading Research and Instruction, 31st Yearbook of the National Reading Conference*, edited by J.A. Niles and L.A. Harris. Rochester, N.Y.: National Reading Conference, 1982.

Cunningham, Patricia, and Cunningham, James. "Content Area Reading-Writing Lessons." *The Reading Teacher* 40 (February 1987): 506-12.

Davey, Beth. "Think Aloud: Modeling the Cognitive Processes of Reading Comprehension." *Journal of Reading* 27 (October 1983): 44-47.

Day, J.D. "Teaching Summarization Skills: A Comparison of Training Methods." Doctoral dissertation, University of Illinois, 1980.

Devine, Thomas. *Teaching Reading Comprehension: From Theory to Practice*. Boston: Allyn & Bacon, 1986.

Hennings, Dorothy Grant. "Essential Reading." *Journal of Reading* 34 (February 1991): 346-53.

Squire, James. "Composing and Comprehending: Two Sides of the Same Basic Process." In *Composing and Comprehending*, edited by Julie Jensen. Urbana, Ill.: National Conference on Research in English, 1984.

Stauffer, Russell. *Teaching Reading as a Thinking Process*. New York: Harper & Row, 1969.

Taylor, B. "Text Structure and Children's Comprehension and Memory for Expository Text." *Journal of Educational Psychology* 74 (1982): 323-40.

APPENDIX A
STUDENT ASSESSMENT

At some point the teacher may wish to assess a student's ability to construct meaning in response to stories, poems, and nonfiction heard or read. One way to do this is by "kidwatching." Here is a guide for kidwatching. To use it, the teacher focuses on the reflective behavior of a child during a literature-based classroom conversation. After the conversation, the teacher records the child's remarks that provide evidence of growth toward the objectives.

In addition, the child keeps a learning log in which he or she responds to stories, poems, and nonfiction by drawing, commenting, and developing schematics. The teacher analyzes the child's entries to determine the ways in which the child is able to interact with a text and then records evidence of the child's growth on the guide.

An Observational Guide for Assessing a Child's Ability To Construct Meaning in Response to Literature

The Objective to Be Assessed	Behavioral Evidence of Growth Toward the Objective
Is the child better able to:	
Prepare for listening to or reading a story, poem, or piece of nonfiction by: • Activating what he/she knows about the content and structure? • Making predictions based on an initial survey of the selection and using those predictions to guide listening and reading? • Raising questions based on an initial survey and listening and reading to answer the questions? Make connections while and after listening to or reading a selection by: • Visualizing and drawing what is described? • Making inferences that go beyond the text and supporting inferences with details from the text? • Developing generalizations based on details provided in a text?	

The Objective to Be Assessed	Behavioral Evidence of Growth Toward the Objective
Is the child better able to:	
• Applying generalizations to the interpretation of new but related situations and problems? • Proposing comparisons and contrasts? • Thinking of related points and examples? • Organizing content by developing a time line, hierarchical schematic, data chart, outline, or map? • Feeling deeply about events, characters, and ideas? Extend ideas met through listening to or reading a selection by: • Developing opinions and judgments and supporting those opinions and judgments with reasons? • Developing creative ideas that go far beyond the text? Monitoring comprehension by employing fix-up strategies?	

APPENDIX B
STUDENT LISTENING LOGS

One way to assess children's interest in listening to and reading stories, poems, and nonfiction is to keep track of their listening and reading preferences. To this end, the children keep their own records of what they enjoyed hearing and reading, listing the titles, date read or heard, and the reasons they liked or did not like the piece.

However, some children have trouble getting started when asked to make notes in a literature log. They may benefit from a guide that provides clues to kinds of thoughts to record. Here are three guides that may help intermediate grade students respond to stories, poems, and nonfiction.

My Personal Literature Log – Story

Use this guide to get started making notes in your "lit" log about a story you have heard or read. You do not have to answer all the questions about any one story. You also may respond in your log by drawing pictures, making a diagram of some kind, or writing sentences.

The name of the story: ______________________________
The author of the story: ______________________________
When I began to read the story: ________________
When I finished it: ________________

My thoughts, predictions, and questions *before* listening or reading

- What is the story going to be about? When does it happen? Where does it take place? Who are the characters? What do I predict will happen?
- What do I know about this time and place and about characters like these?
- What do I know about this author and the things he or she generally writes?

My thoughts, feelings, predictions, and questions *while* listening or reading

- Are my predictions right? Who are the characters? Where and when does the story take place? What causes conflict, or tension, in the story? What happens to get the story going? What happens as a result? What happens after that?
- Do I see a pattern developing in the story? Can I use this pattern to predict what will happen?
- What do I predict this character will do next? What evidence do I have that supports my prediction?
- How does this character feel? How do I know he or she feels this way? How do I feel as a result?
- Is what is happening fair? Bad? Good? What would I have done in the same situation?
- Will there be a happy ending? Why? Why not?

My thoughts *after* listening or reading

- What did I learn from the story? How did I feel at the end? (Perhaps draw a word web of ideas and feelings, or fingerpaint a picture filled with feelings.)
- Was there a pattern to the story? (Perhaps draw a diagram or story map that shows the pattern.)
- When did something similar happen to me? (Perhaps write a story with a similar pattern or theme, or similar characters.)
- Does this story remind me of another story? In what way? (Perhaps make a comparison chart.)
- What did I like or dislike about the story? (Perhaps write an opinion paragraph and tell why.)

My Personal Literature Log – Poetry

Use this guide to help you get started making notes in your "lit" log about a poem you have heard or read. You do not have to answer all the questions about any one poem. You also may respond in your log by drawing pictures, making a diagram of some kind, or writing sentences.

The name of the poem: ______________________________
The author of the poem: ______________________________

My thoughts, predictions, and questions *before* listening or reading

- What is this poem going to be about?
- What do I already know about the topic of the poem?
- What do I know about the author, other poems he or she has written, and the kind of poem he or she generally writes?

My thoughts, feelings, predictions, and questions *while* listening or reading

- What words or lines do I particularly like? Why do these appeal to me?
- What words or lines do I not like? Why do these not appeal to me?
- What is the poet trying to say to me?

My thoughts *after* listening or reading

- Is there a pattern to the poem? What is it? (Perhaps write your own poem with the pattern.)
- How does the poem make me feel? (Perhaps draw a picture that expresses the feeling.)
- What meaning does this poem hold for me? (Perhaps make a web of words that come to mind.)
- When have I thought or felt in a similar way? (Perhaps write a story that tells about it.)
- Of what other poem or story does this one remind me? (Perhaps make a chart that compares the pieces.)
- What kinds of thoughts do I have on this topic? (Perhaps write your own poem that expresses your idea or follows the pattern of the poem you have heard or read.)

My Personal Literature Log – Nonfiction

Use this guide to help you get started making notes in your "lit" log about a piece of nonfiction you have heard or read. You do not have to answer all the questions about any one selection. You also may respond in your log by drawing pictures, making a diagram of some kind, or writing sentences.

The name of the selection: ______________________________
The author of the selection: ______________________________
When I began to read the selection: ________________
When I finished it: ________________

My thoughts, predictions, and questions *before* listening or reading

- What is this selection going to be about?
- What do I already know about that topic?
- What questions will this selection answer for me?

My thoughts, feelings, predictions, and questions *while* listening or reading

- What information am I getting to answer my questions? (Refer to your before-reading questions and try answering them as you go along.)
- What is the order of events if there is one? (Perhaps make a timeline to record events.)
- What are the important terms to learn? (Perhaps draw equations that show terms and definitions.)
- What are the main ideas? What are the important supporting details? (Perhaps draw a visual that shows the main ideas and the supporting details.)
- How do the ideas fit together? (Perhaps map the ideas.)

My thoughts *after* listening or reading

- What did I learn? (Write a summary paragraph.)
- What was not clear to me? What do I not understand? (Go back and read again.)
- How does this information relate to other things I know? (Perhaps make a summary web, a chart, or some other visual that shows the way the information fits together.)
- Was this information interesting to me? Why? Why not? (Perhaps write a paragraph giving your reasons.)
- How can I use this information? (Perhaps identify related examples.)